D1437150

CRITICAL GUIDES TO SPANISH TEXTS

4

Gallegos: Doña Bárbara

CRITICAL GUIDES TO SPANISH TEXTS

Edited by

J. E. Varey and A. D. Deyermond

GALLEGOS

DOÑA BÁRBARA

*

D. L. SHAW

Senior Lecturer in Hispanic Studies
University of Edinburgh

Grant & Cutler Ltd

in association with

Tamesis Books Ltd

1972

Depósito legal: M.-11.312-1972

Printed in Spain by Talleres Gráficos de Ediciones Castilla, S.A.

Maestro Alonso, 23 - Madrid

for

GRANT & CUTLER LTD
11 BUCKÍNGHAM STREET, LONDON W.C.2.

Contents

For Mariella

Foreword

Doña Bárbara is possibly the most famous Latin-American novel, to judge by the number of translations and editions which have appeared. Its author, Rómulo Gallegos, was born in Caracas in 1884. Forced by financial hardship to abandon his university studies, he became a teacher in Caracas until the success of *Doña Bárbara* made him famous. He was then nominated to the Senate by the ruling dictator, Juan Vicente Gómez, but proudly resigned and went into exile. After Gómez's death in 1935 Gallegos went back to Venezuela to begin a political career which culminated in his election as President of the Republic in 1948. Less than a year later he was removed by a military coup and spent almost ten years more in exile before returning again. He died in 1969.

Doña Bárbara, the third and greatest of Gallegos' nine published novels, appeared in 1929 when the author was forty-four. It belongs to what a critic has called the "seis de la fama", the six most successful Latin-American novels published in the first thirty years of this century. Three of them, *Don Segundo Sombra* by Ricardo Güiraldes (Argentina), *La vorágine* by José Eustasio Rivera (Colombia) and *Doña Bárbara* itself, are the classic examples of the Latin-American *novela de la tierra.* Their successful incorporation into fiction of the striking natural background, the *pampa,* the *selva* and the *llano* of the subcontinent, represented an important break with the imitation of European models and a great stride forward towards authenticity in Latin-American literature. *Doña Bárbara,* the best known of the three, marks the peak of achievement in Latin-American fiction before the emergence of the so-called *nueva novela* in the 1950s. Its place in Latin-American literature is permanent.

Chapter I

Origin of the Theme

The crisis of confidence which overtook Spain after her disastrous defeat in the Cuban War of 1898 was not confined to the Peninsula. Paradoxically the countries of Latin America were overtaken by a similar crisis. They, who might have been expected to see the final overthrow of Spanish power in the New World as the dawn of a new age of progress there, seem instead to have shared in the humiliation inflicted on the Motherland. This was no doubt partly due to a prophetic realization that the decisive intervention of the United States was the prelude to an era of economic dominance by the Colossus of the North.

But there was also an interior process of demoralization. The emergence after 1810 of the Latin-American sub-continent from colonial status to political independence had been originally accompanied by an upsurge of optimism about the destiny of the area and the potential of its citizens. A new sense of their own worth had begun to show itself among Latin-Americans. Clear signs of this spirit of confidence and optimism can be seen in the work of such men as the Venezuelan Andrés Bello and the Argentinian Mariano Moreno. But before long Bolívar, the great Liberator himself, was writing:

> There is no good faith in America, nor among the nations of America. Treaties are scraps of paper; constitutions, printed matter; elections, battles; freedom, anarchy; and life a torment. Such, Fellow Americans, is our deplorable situation. Unless we change it death is to be preferred.[1]

As anarchy, civil war and dictatorship followed the achievement of

[1]'Panoramic View of Spanish America', in *Selected Writings*, II, (New York, 1951), p. 747.

independence, barbarism appeared to have triumphed. Optimism and confidence gave way abruptly to acute pessimism.

The figure who above all embodied the crisis of Latin-American self-confidence in the mid-nineteenth century was the great Argentinian writer-president Domingo F. Sarmiento (1811-1888). His masterpiece *Facundo* (1845)[2] is the first major attempt to examine the Latin-American problem in depth. Recognizing what the emergence of violence and dictatorship in Argentina could mean, Sarmiento boldly sub-titled his work 'Civilización y barbarie'. *Facundo* remains a great seminal work. It is the direct forerunner of Gallegos' *Doña Bárbara.* But it set a fashion for interpreting the Latin-American problem, not in terms of political, social or economic conditions, but in terms of mentality, racial heritage, or what Spanish expressively calls *modo de ser.*

Sarmiento's postulate of a Latin-American *intra-personalidad* existing in a state of perpetual tension between civilization and barbarism is interesting but unverifiable. It has led to arbitrary counter-assertions such as those of José Enrique Rodó (Uruguay) in *Ariel* (1900) and José Vasconcelos (Mexico) in *La raza cósmica* (1925). Harking back to Bello and Moreno these writers attempt to defend the Latin-American *modo de ser* on grounds no less questionable than those on which Sarmiento had attacked it. Also, while intellectual opinion has been busy considering the Latin-American *modo de ser* in the abstract, as if it were a changeless prior entity governing progress in Latin America, attention has been deflected from the practical task of creating conditions which are likely to alter it. More will be said about this in dealing with Gallegos' treatment of the theme in *Doña Bárbara* itself.

For the moment it is sufficient to sketch his own early views on

---

[2]See Cyril Jones' forthcoming study in this series of Sarmiento's *Facundo o Civilización y barbarie.*

the Latin-American problem[3], which by the beginning of the twentieth century was entering a new phase of discussion. Darío's famous 'Salutación del optimista' which appeared in *Cantos de vida y esperanza* (1905) caught the mood of the times exactly. The poem calls on the Hispanic peoples both in Europe and America to cast off "pálidas indolencias" and "desconfianzas fatales" in order to march forward together towards the triumph of *hispanidad*. Shortly before, Rodó, to whom *Cantos de vida y esperanza* was dedicated, had written reassuringly in *Ariel* of "una herencia de raza . . . vínculo sagrado que nos une a inmortales páginas de la historia" and had confidently prophesied the proximity of "la América que nosotros soñamos". But the old problem of barbarism remained and was soon to reappear as tangibly as ever in the horrors of the Mexican Revolution. With it survived the old insecurity and doubt as to the worth of Latin-American nationality. Carlos Octavio Bunge (Argentina) in *Nuestra América* (1903), Alcides Arguedas (Bolivia) in *Pueblo enfermo* (1909), and José Ingenieros (Argentina) in *La evolución de las ideas argentinas* (1918) all gave memorable expression to a negative view of what Bunge called "el genio de la raza".

Of the three classic nineteenth-century solutions to the problems besetting Latin-America —legislation, immigration and education— the first two appeared by this time to have failed. Education remained, and it was to this that Gallegos turned in 1901. It led him back inevitably to Sarmiento, the great educator, and thus to the conflict of civilization and barbarism. In his important early essay 'Necesidad de valores culturales' (August 1912) Gallegos' reference is specific:

> Si quisiéramos sintetizar en un esquema la diferencia característica que hay entre estos dos señalados síntomas de enfermedades sociales [Gallegos is referring to *huelgas* and *montoneras*] y al mismo

---

[3]Indispensable for this and other aspects of Gallegos' thought is the collection of his early essays and later speeches and lectures entitled *Una posición en la vida* (Mexico, 1954).

tiempo referirlos a sus orígenes, podríamos expresarla con estos
dos términos antitéticos: la ciudad y el monte, con lo que deter-
minaríamos, no sólo los lugares en que suelen suceder, sino también
su naturaleza propia, las circunstancias que los producen, el
espíritu y las tendencias que los animan, que es como decir:
civilización y barbarie [Gallegos' italics].

Gallegos' early writings, especially 'Las causas' (February 1909), make
it clear that like Sarmiento and many others he presupposed the
existence in Venezuela of a *modo de ser,* what he called *el alma de la
raza,* with mainly negative characteristics leading to self-perpetuating
barbarism. He tended to make the traditional mistake of regarding
this *alma* as a kind of mystical entity, existing separately from
economic and social conditions and in some way determining their
development. Progress thus comes to be seen as dependent chiefly
on the possibility of redeeming the *alma de la raza,* and it is here that
Gallegos' essays on education assume their true significance.

The answer for Gallegos at this stage was not, as in Sarmiento,
more education, but a different kind of education, designed to
combat the vices of the *alma de la raza.* He advocated a pattern of
teaching modelled on Anglo-Saxon practices, intended to develop
character as well as to impart knowledge. Much of Gallegos' adult
life was spent serving this ideal as a teacher. But it must be regarded
as naive. Educational systems tend to reflect their social context. It
is social change which brings about educational change rather than
vice versa. Possibly this is one of the reasons which induced Gallegos
to associate himself in later life with a left-of-centre political movement.

However, the more closely Gallegos' early ideology is examined,
the more obvious becomes his ambivalent attitude to the interpretation of the Venezuelan *modo de ser.* It is impossible to overlook
the contradictions which appear in his early essays concerned with
this. Within a month of writing in 'Las causas' that the Venezuelan
national character is amorphous, hybrid and utterly incapable of

providing a basis for solid and stable social progress, we find him confidently asserting in 'La alianza hispanoamericana' that the future lies, not with the decadent races of Europe, but with "el vigor juvenil de las [razas] que se levantan en nuestro continente". In August of the same year ('Necesidad de valores culturales', 1909) we find the even more specific statement that "Barbarie quiere decir juventud, y juventud es fuerza, promesa y esperanza".

His short story 'Los aventureros' (1913), often mentioned as pre-figuring *Doña Bárbara* because of its use of the theme of barbarism versus civilization, illustrates the position as it affected his creative writing. In the story Gallegos borrows from nineteenth-century European literature the idea of using a railway as a symbol of progress and modern life. Thus the track under construction represents civilization moving outwards from the city. Matías Rosalía and his band of guerrillas, who harass the railway project and try to prevent its advance, represent barbarism. The key-sentence is that which describes Rosalía and his men as revealing "la única energía de la raza, blindada de barbarie pero íntegra, pura como un metal nativo". Here in Gallegos' mystique *el alma de la raza* is no longer completely negative. It has become something unspoilt and solid, potentially useful and valuable. Thus the foundations are laid for Santos Luzardo's eventual discovery of the worth of barbarism and for the ambivalence which runs right through *Doña Bárbara.*

Gallegos' first major novel, *Reinaldo Solar* (written 1913, published 1920), reveals that he was still facing an unresolved crisis in his sense of nationality. While he specifically compares the Venezuelan people in the book to "el feto de una nación abortada" and refers directly to "el alma abolida de nuestra raza", he elsewhere includes a mention of the hidden beauty of "el alma ignorada y hermética de nuestra raza". The answer seemed to come to him with his next novel *La trepadora* (1925). Hilario Guanipa, the illegitimate son of the wealthy patrician don Jaime del Casal and a local peasant girl, prospers and marries back into the landed élite. He and his daughter Victoria, who in her turn marries a del Casal, show Gallegos feeling his way towards the symbolic figure of racial and social synthesis which he was to achieve rather more effectively in Marisela of *Doña Bárbara.* ·

Circumstances of Composition

Encouraged by the favourable reception accorded to *La trepadora,* Gallegos presently began work on a new novel. The original plan of the narrative envisaged a brief trip by the central character from Caracas to San Fernando de Apure, and Gallegos was anxious to visit the area himself in order to describe it convincingly. Providentially in Holy Week of 1927 he was invited to a hunting party at the ranch of La Candelaria, some forty miles south of San Fernando. It is important to notice that this was Gallegos' first visit to the *llano* and that it was extremely short. Gallegos was in full-time employment as a teacher. The school holidays lasted seven days, two of which were spent in reaching La Candelaria owing to a breakdown of the car Gallegos was using. Another day was spent on the return journey. Gallegos' visit therefore lasted exactly four days. The belief that he spent a long period living the life of the *llano* and documenting himself by first-hand experience is unfounded.

His stay was sufficient, however, to fire his imagination. The earlier story was put aside and Gallegos spent the short time feverishly collecting material for a novel set entirely in the *llano* region. The process has been described by the novelist himself both in the preface 'Como conocí a Doña Bárbara' to the twenty-fifth anniversary edition of *Doña Bárbara* (Mexico, 1954, pp.7-13), in 'La pura mujer sobre la tierra' (*Una posición en la vida*; see note 3) and in conversation with J. E. Englekirk whose article in *Hispania* is of major importance.[4] Gallegos was greatly assisted by a certain Sr. Rodríguez and especially by Antonio José Torrealba Osto who appears in the

[4]For this and other references see the Bibliographical Note at the end.

novel as Antonio Sandoval. Most of the secondary figures in the novel and all the principal characters except Santos Luzardo, Marisela and possibly Colonel Apolinar were directly inspired by local people in the area of La Candelaria. Gallegos referred to them as "documentos vivientes" and wrote in the 1954 preface already mentioned:

> A Juan Primito y sus rebullones, tonto y bueno, lo conocí en un pueblo de los valles del Tuy. Y a los de contraria índole: Mujiquita y Pernalete, Balbino Paiba y El Brujeador, me los encontré en varios sitios de mi país, componiendo personificaciones de la tragedia venezolana (26).[5]

They can for the most part be quite definitely identified. The same is true of many of the place-names and a number of the incidents.

Among the latter, of major importance are the family feud between the Luzardos and the Barqueros, which was suggested to Gallegos by a well-known struggle between two local families, and part of the life-story of Doña Bárbara herself. The model for her appears to have been one Francisca Vásquez, "Doña Pancha", who around the turn of the century had possessed a large tract of land about a hundred miles from La Candelaria. Though Gallegos never met her (she appears to have died in the early 1920s), her ability to compete with any male *llanero* in his work or in knowledge of the region, and her propensity for engaging in violent disputes over land-boundaries, were already sufficiently legendary to fix her indelibly in his mind. Moreover the fact that she was reputed to have had a daughter in spite of her masculine manner of life must have suggested irresistibly to Gallegos the situation of Marisela in the novel.

At all events, during his journey back to Caracas, Gallegos seems to have had the initial inspiration for the theme of *Doña Bárbara*: the conflict of civilization and barbarism. As we have seen, this was not a new theme to him since it had appeared both in his essays and in 'Los aventureros'. Indeed it can be said to underlie his whole

[5]All references are to the Caracas 1964 edition of *Doña Bárbara* based on that of Mexico 1954: these are the only completely reliable texts. Henceforth each reference gives the Part and chapter number followed by the page.

personal ideology. Now it suddenly took fictional shape in terms of a new plot. Gallegos poured it out white hot in twenty-eight days and began to have it printed by the Tipografía Vargas for the Caracas publishing house Elite. This was the first draft. But when the first *pliego* had been printed the student rebellion of the 28th February 1928 broke out. Gallegos, either disappointed by the appearance of the work in print or fearing that it would not be allowed to circulate in such troubled times, ordered the printing to be stopped and the existing *pliego* to be destroyed. Friends who had heard this draft (then entitled *La Coronela*) read to them by Gallegos declared subsequently that it was a very inferior product compared to *Doña Bárbara* as we know it.

Worries of a domestic nature then intervened. The novelist's wife, doña Teotiste, had developed a condition which required surgical treatment. The couple decided to have the operation carried out in Bologna, Italy, and set out by ship for Europe. During the voyage, Gallegos, lacking confidence in his new novel, wished to dump the manuscript of *La Coronela* into the Atlantic, but was dissuaded by doña Teotiste. This was not her only contribution to the novel. In the original version Santos was already married and travelled to the *llanos* with his wife. Only after her death did the idyll with Marisela begin. Doña Teotiste, to whom Gallegos habitually read his work, wisely objected to this first marriage of Santos and Gallegos cut it out. During her convalescence, in the summer and autumn of 1928, partly in Italy and partly in Spain, Gallegos revised and re-wrote much of the material of *La Coronela.* Under its new title, *Doña Bárbara*, he submitted the work to a publishing house in Barcelona, Araluce, who accepted it on terms rather disadvantageous to the author. He received 800 copies as his share of the bargain.

The first edition, of 2000 copies, came out on 15 February 1929. It was an immense success. In September it was acclaimed as the best novel of the month in Spanish by a jury which included Gabriel

Miró, Pérez de Ayala and Gómez de Baquero. Gallegos returned to Spain in November 1929 and again extensively re-wrote the work before it came out in a second edition. This second edition (Barcelona, Araluce, January 1930) is the novel as we now know it. Close on sixty editions have since appeared. It has been translated into sixteen languages in Europe and the Middle East. It has also been filmed, rather disappointingly, in Mexico with María Félix as doña Bárbara, the script being written by Gallegos himself. In 1967 an opera based on the novel was staged in Caracas. No other Latin-American novel has yet achieved equal success.

Textual Revision of 1929-30

Between the first Araluce edition of *Doña Bárbara* in 1929 and the second in 1930, Gallegos made drastic changes to the novel.[6] Briefly they were as follows. The division of the novel into its three parts was altered and the old chapters, most of which were modified or partly re-written, were grouped in a different order. The results can be tabulated as follows:

Part I

1929 edition		1930 edition	
Chapter I	----------	I	
Chapter II	----------	II	
Chapter III	----------	IV	
Chapter IV	----------	V	
Chapter V	----------	VII	
Chapter VI	----------	VI	(with new title: 'El recuerdo de Asdrúbal', borrowed from old chapter VII)
Chapter VII	----------	III	(with new title: 'La devoradora de hombres')
Chapters VIII-XIII	-------	VIII-XIII	

Part II

1929 edition	1930 edition	
Part III, chapter III, in part ---	I	(with new title: 'Un acontecimiento insólito')

---

[6] A detailed account of these changes by the present writer will appear in a forthcoming number of *Hispanic Review*.

Chapter	I	II
Chapter	IX, in part	III

Chapter   I ---------- II
Chapter   IX, in part ------ III (with new title: 'Los rebu-llones')
Chapter   IX, in part ------ V (with new title: 'Las mudanzas de doña Bárbara')
Chapter   IV ---------- IV
Chapter   II, in part ------ VI (with new title: 'El espanto del bramador')
Chapter   II, in part ------ VII
Chapter   III ---------- VIII
Chapter   V ---------- IX
Chapter   VI ---------- X
Chapter VII ---------- XI
Chapter VIII ---------- XII
Chapter   IX, in part ------ XIII

Part III

Here, after the addition of 'El espanto de la sabana' (formerly Part II, Chapter V) as chapter I, the order of the chapters is unchanged with one exception. Chapters VII and VIII of the 1929 edition ('Los retozos de Míster Danger' and 'La gloria roja') change places, becoming in 1930 chapters IX and VIII respectively.

*   *   *

The consequences of these structural alterations are three-fold. First, the division of the novel into its three constituent parts is rendered more justifiable. The chapters which now open Parts II and III mark definite articulations of the narrative in a way which was not previously the case. Second, the arrangement of the episodes is now more logical and emphasizes more clearly the parallelism or duality Santos/doña Bárbara which is the novel's basic structural principle. Third, unwieldy chapters of the 1929 edition, such as Part II chapters II and IX, are broken up into their constituent parts, and wholly new episodes such as Santos' first interview with Pernalete and Primito's first visit to Altamira are added.

In terms of character, Santos' original inherent repressed barbarism is softened to become something much more like tough manliness while Bárbara's rôle is expanded so that her character receives a firmer outline and advances in stature and dignity. Primito's rôle is hugely expanded and important modifications affect Paiba, Carmelito and Pajarote. Significantly, the least affected part of the original version is the affair between Santos and Marisela, which is hardly touched at all in the revision.

Finally, the text is expanded by about 20 per cent, with additions and suppressions on almost every page, many of them of signal importance. The expansion of the text was not consistent, however. About 8000 words were added to Part I, about 9000 to Part II, but only about 3000 to Part III. In general the result is a vast improvement with which Gallegos was clearly satisfied, for when in 1954 he once more revised the book the changes he then made merely concerned differences of paragraphing and small verbal details.

Theme

In the majority of serious novels it is the theme which most clearly conveys the author's insight and thereby indicates the deeper meaning underlying the story. At the same time the theme governs the selection of episodes; it shapes the plot and gives it a recognizable direction. Without a theme the novel is left with a mere subject, appealing to the reader's interest or curiosity but suggesting little that is significant about human life and behaviour. Where theme becomes too prominent, arbitrarily distorting the events and characterization, the work becomes a thesis-novel. It attempts to impose on us an aggressive point of view to which the author is committed. Instead of seeking to explore reality, the writer tries to alter it.

It is from the theme, therefore, that a critical consideration of *Doña Bárbara* is best begun. What that theme is we already know. Gallegos is concerned with the treacherous heritage of the Latin-American personality, the menacing attraction of barbarism and the constant threat it presents to *sociabilidad* and civilization. The origins and development of this theme have been briefly described. It remains to examine the treatment which it receives in the novel itself.

Gallegos handles the theme in three main ways. First, the conflict of civilization and barbarism is seen in practical, material terms of the struggle to modernize the *llano*. Secondly, it is seen in human— and at the same time symbolic— terms of the confrontation which occurs between the hero, Santos, and doña Bárbara. Thirdly, it is seen in individual terms: those of Santos' struggle with himself. This triple approach to the theme is important in that it constitutes a useful element of variety. It not only allows Gallegos to deflect the reader's interest at will from one aspect of the problem to another, it also ensures that each deflection tends to produce a gain in emphasis as one feature underlines another. At the same time it tends to conceal the limitations imposed by the theme on Gallegos' choice of incidents, while bringing out the complexity underlying the simple antithesis: civilization versus barbarism.

In turn, it is this complexity of theme which saves the novel from becoming a work of thesis. Most novels of ideas are usually only one step away from this currently unfashionable category, and *Doña Bárbara* is at first sight no exception. But the multiple focus which Gallegos uses permits him to avoid the obtrusively unilateral, blinkered approach of the conventional thesis novelist. In addition account must be taken of the inconsistencies of Gallegos' outlook explored on an earlier page. Of the three aspects of the theme, only the first is seen unambiguously. The importance of material progress to the *llano* is never questioned. Gallegos clearly assumes that under-development and resistance to change are unqualified evils and makes no attempt to idealize them as Güiraldes, for example, implicitly does in *Don Segundo Sombra,* the great novel of the Argentinian plains. The second and third aspects of the theme, on the other hand, are presented ambivalently. This is in line with Gallegos' growing reluctance to interpret the Venezuelan *alma de la raza* in negative terms as he had done in his earliest work, and with his consequent unwillingness to see the heritage of barbarism, which in his view had

G didn't write just to record their identity/
its hasto- he wrote to galvanize
change

shaped that *alma,* as something wholly bad. Having now evolved to a position from which he saw a definite connection between barbarism and the hidden reserve of energy of the race, its youthful vitality, Gallegos now tends to present barbarism, whether personified in doña Bárbara or lurking in Santos' inner personality, as something not wholly unattractive.

Initially however, Gallegos, through the mouth of Santos, presents *barbarie* in strictly practical terms. The key-phrase occurs in Part I, chapter II, as Santos travels thoughtfully through the *llano* towards Altamira: "Lo que urge es modificar las circunstancias" (54). A confrontation at the human level with doña Bárbara (the subject of the rest of the book) is here, interestingly enough, specifically rejected: "¿De qué serviría acabar con el cacicazgo de doña Bárbara en el Arauca? Reaparecería más allá bajo otro nombre" (54). Barbarism is presented, not in human terms, but as arising from the surroundings: *insalubridad* (the endemic marsh-fever which has killed off Melesio's sons), flood, drought, the desert; in brief, as something produced by the natural environment itself. Civilization thus becomes a question of taming the plains by bringing people to them: the old nineteenth-century Argentinian slogan "civilizar es poblar". The difficulty is that of attracting settlers to so inhospitable a region.

This is Gallegos' first formulation of the problem and its solution. It reappears at intervals throughout the rest of the novel, centring on two experiments which Santos undertakes: the setting up of the *queseras* and the *cerca*. Both are deliberately presented in a semi-symbolic way. Just as Santos' efforts are basically directed at civilizing the savage human inhabitants of the *llano,* so the cheese-making shed is erected as part of a conscious design to civilize the savage cattle, to "suprimir ferocidad" at the animal level. Hence the careful notation in Part II, chapter XII, that "la quesera comenzaba así la civilización de la barbarie del ganado" (310). The collapse of the experiment when Jesusito is killed by the tiger is, of course, merely a temporary setback, as we perceive from the eventual triumph of the *cerca*.

This in turn is just as directly associated with the theme of the novel. "Por ella", Santos asserts, "empezaría la civilización de la llanura" (I, xii, 165). As the people are converted, as the cattle are tamed, so the land itself must submit to the civilizing restraint of enclosure, which Santos compares to the restraining influence of principles on human conduct. So, on the last page of the novel, it is the erection of the wire fences which symbolizes the marking out of a single straight road to the (civilized) future. The fact that Antonio, the typical plainsman, at first rejects the idea of enclosures, but later accepts it —with the inevitable comment by Gallegos: "Era la idea del civilizador, germinando ya en el cerebro del hombre de la rutina" (III, ii, 344) to drive home the point— completes the coherence of the pattern. To civilize one aspect of the *llano* is to contribute directly to civilizing the rest.

Criticism of this aspect of the theme must centre on its limited objectives and its subordinate position in relation to the other two aspects. The fundamental problem of the Venezuelan *llano* was and remains that of poverty and economic underdevelopment, combined with *latifundia* (extensive landholding) by single owners. It is probable that this situation is at the root of rural *barbarie* in so far as it has existed, and not (as Gallegos appears to assume) vice-versa. If it is so, the remedy for barbarism can lie only in radical agrarian reform, which is unlikely without prior social reform and a change in power-groups over the country as a whole. Cottage-industry (the *quesera*), enclosures (the *cerca*) and the rise of "buen cacicazgo" in place ,of the selfish and corrupt authority of doña Bárbara and Pernalete (Gallegos' implicit suggestion) are hardly more than trivial palliatives. It must be recalled, of course, that the action of the novel is supposed to take place around the year 1910[7] when this

[7]See the phrase "desde el '90 hacia acá" in Part I, chapter V (suppressed in

was perhaps all that was objectively possible. When Gallegos became President of Venezuela in 1948 he advocated radical reforms.

Hardly has the socio-economic problem been enunciated', however, when at the end of Part I, chapter II it is suddenly reinterpreted in terms of Santos' need to "luchar contra doña Bárbara, creatura y personificación de los tiempos que corrían" (55). This becomes a struggle, not with physical elements and practical problems, but with an outlook personified in a human figure: Bárbara. Already Santos' first positive reaction has been against a man, Melquíades, at the *palodeagua* in chapter I, not against a practical problem. So now increasingly the theme is expressed as Santos' fight against people, their outlook and customs, rather than against adverse physical and social conditions. His second reaction is similarly against a man, Paiba, whom he "tames" symbolically before taming the animal, the horse, in Part I, chapter VIII, which (like the cattle in the *queseras*) represents the *barbarie* of nature. Subsequently he goes on to tame the Mondragones, Ño Pernalete and Danger, while at the same time altering the outlook of the 'good' *llanero*-figure Antonio Sandoval, before doña Bárbara finally capitulates.

This shift from conditions to *modo de ser* finds its justification in fictional expediency. The dramatic effect of a conflict of personalities is much greater, and generates much more identification and suspense in the reader, than a conflict between a hero and external circumstances. Also of course there is a close relationship between the outlook of people and their physical and economic environment. Santos decides to break the vicious circle —of bad conditions producing *barbarie* of outlook which perpetuates bad conditions— at the human point first, because it suits Gallegos's fictional purposes that he should.

But the gain in fictional effect is not fully exploited, and it is in

the 1954 revision) and Santos' "hace veinte años" (II, xii, 308) referring back to about 1890. See also the reference to the Cuban War and the disaster of 1898 taking place in Santos' early teens.

any case bought at some cost. It is not fully exploited because, although the two antithetical forces in the novel are personified in Santos and Bárbara, they never meet directly. How much more interesting would the novel have been if Santos had felt the attraction of Bárbara as he eventually feels the attraction of what she personifies: the *barbarie* of the *llano*! But he never does. They meet only six times, are alone only three times, and have only one significant dialogue (II, v, 247-253). Gallegos baulks at the logical consequence of shifting the presentation of the theme into human terms.

By presenting the theme in this way Gallegos implicitly accepts that the human problem does in fact come first: changing people must take precedence over changing conditions. But the modern tendency is to think in the opposite terms: it is by altering the environment that one hopes to alter people. Again, what is it that actually triumphs? Is it the application of Santos' "ideales de civilizado" to the human context of the *llano*? Hardly. What triumphs is his *hombría,* not his principles, his perseverance, his technical know-how nor his capital investment. A very dangerous doctrine is implicit here, underlined by the contrast between Lorenzo Barquero and Santos. Significantly, it is Lorenzo who enunciates the key-principle: "Es necesario matar al centauro" (I, x, 142), but he lacks the personality to put it into effect. Santos merely inherits the ideology of his older cousin, but he possesses the strength of character to make it work even if its purity is compromised in the process. Unlike the struggle of Santos with the physical environment, the struggle with the human one reveals the triumph of one form of force, which happens to be allied to what Gallegos approves of, over another form which he deprecates. Does the end justify the means?

The third aspect of the theme is the struggle of Santos with himself, with what Gallegos in fine positivistic nineteenth-century fashion regards as being "en la sangre"[8]. This is unquestionably the

[8] See the surviving reference in Part II, chapter XII to "la indolencia del indio

most effective, gripping and convincing of the author's three methods of approach to *civilización y barbarie*. If it is Santos' struggle with Bárbara which provides the drama of the novel, it is his private conflict which provides the illusion of psychological depth. It will be explored in the later treatment of Santos' evolution.

Influences

The basic narrative pattern of *Doña Bárbara* can be traced to the famous passage at the end of Balzac's *Le père Goriot* in which the youthful Rastignac resolves to conquer the capital, triumphing over its social obstacles. His rôle illustrates a theme which was to be widely exploited by later novelists: that of the provincial stripling pitting himself against the metropolis. In Spain Galdós began his career as a novelist by using this theme in *La Fontana de Oro* (1870). It also appears memorably in Pereda's *Pedro Sánchez* (1883) as it had in Latin America with the Chilean Alberto Blest Gana's *Martín Rivas* twenty years before. But the time quickly came when the primary possibilities of the theme were exhausted and a new twist had to be given to it. This was done quite simply by turning it upside down. In two famous antithetical novels, *Doña Perfecta* and *Peñas arriba,* Galdós and Pereda described the experiences of a young man from the capital who ventures into the provinces. Galdós describes the triumph of violence and fanaticism over the progressive ideas of his hero, Pepe Rey. In Pereda's novel, on the other hand, an idle young *madrileño* is gradually converted into an enlightened and useful country proprietor. Gallegos resolves optimistically the antithesis established by the contrasting ideologies of Pereda and Galdós which, in his case, takes the form of the *civilización-barbarie* motif already discussed. In order to give it convincing fictional expression Gallegos grafts it on to the established narrative pattern provided by the

que llevamos en la sangre" (309) and the reference in the 1929 edition, p. 99 —later suppressed— to "El impulsivo que [Santos] llevaba en la sangre".

European novel. The young man from the capital, Santos, represents civilization; doña Bárbara incarnates the barbarism of the provincial *llano*.

In the matter of more specific influences two earlier novels are regularly mentioned in connection with *Doña Bárbara*. One is *La vorágine* by José Eustasio Rivera (Colombia), published in 1924; the other is Galdós' *Doña Perfecta* itself (1876). Comparison of *Doña Bárbara* and *La vorágine* need not detain us long. The first point of interest is the fact that the hero of *La vorágine*, Arturo Cova, is, like Santos Luzardo, a city-bred intellectual visiting the interior of the country. But as we have just seen this fictional situation originated in the nineteenth century. The second feature is the appearance in *La vorágine* of madona Zoraida, a middle-aged harpy with attributes slightly similar to those of doña Bárbara. Given the great success of *La vorágine*, an element of influence cannot be completely ruled out, though Gallegos specifically denied it. But we know that the real model for doña Bárbara was doña Pancha Vásquez and it seems unnecessary to look for any further source of inspiration. In any case the masculine-type woman is a stock figure of books and films dealing with life in primitive conditions.

The possible influence of Galdós, however, deserves to be considered in greater detail. That Galdós was among the authors whom Gallegos read and deeply admired during his formative years is an undisputed fact. *Doña Perfecta* is possibly Galdós' most widely read and discussed novel. There can be no question that Gallegos had read it. When we place it beside *Doña Bárbara* three features in common immediately stand out.

First of all the basic pattern and structure of the two novels are curiously similar. In each a young intellectual from the capital returns to a region in the provinces where he has some run-down property. Through a series of illustrative experiences he becomes aware of an existing situation of *barbarie* which he resolves to change.

The hero's main antagonist is in each case a woman of striking character flanked by a group of unscrupulous supporters. Though unencumbered by husbands (doña Perfecta is a widow) each of these women has a daughter, a cousin of the hero, with whom he falls in love. The main difference is the ending. Though the final situation is in each case basically similar (the hero's life is threatened by one of the antagonist's henchmen), it is resolved differently in the two novels. While Pepe Rey is shot by Caballuco, Santos escapes and marries Marisela. Here the contrasting outlooks of Galdós and Gallegos come into play.

The second feature is the evolution of the two heroes[9]. Each is at the outset a representative of civilization. But each gradually becomes tainted with *barbarie.* This is a major point of similarity, so far overlooked by critics. In the important scene between Pepe and doña Perfecta in chapter XIX, Pepe, like Santos, announces his shift of attitude, the triumph of barbarism: "Este espectáculo, esta injusticia, esta violencia inaudita es la que *convierte mi rectitud en barbarie,* mi razón en fuerza, mi honradez en violencia." Fully conscious, like Santos, of the evolution he is undergoing, Pepe exclaims: "Era razonable, y soy un bruto; era respetuoso y soy insolente; era culto y me encuentro salvaje." Thirdly, comparing their respective positions he declares to doña Perfecta: "Hemos venido a ser tan *bárbaro* el uno como el otro."[10] It is impossible to mistake the parallelism, visible not only in the narrative structure but also in the development of Pepe and Santos in the two novels.

Three other possible influences remain to be mentioned briefly. As long ago as 1929 Julio Planchart in an essay reprinted in *Temas críticos* (Caracas, 1948) compared *Doña Bárbara* with Emilia Pardo Bazán's *Los pazos de Ulloa* (1886), emphasizing the similarity between

[9]Cf. J. E. Varey's analysis of *Doña Perfecta* in this series. D. T. Sisto, 'Doña Perfecta and Doña Bárbara', *Hispania,* 37 (1954), 167-170, deals chiefly with the similarities between the two women.
[10]The italics in the above quotations from Galdós are my own.

Primitivo in the latter and both Paiba and El Brujeador in the former.
More recently A. Chapman has implied a suspiciously close parallel
between Marisela and Bret Harte's M'liss. Finally A. S. Michalski
sees in Zola's *Nana* (1888) the source of the phrase "la devoradora
de hombres" and of the La Catira episode in Part II of *Doña Bárbara.*

Chapter II

From the standpoint of fictional technique the striking feature of *Doña Bárbara* is the rigid consistency with which the theme conditions and indeed dominates the remaining elements of the narrative. The text, as we have already seen, was re-written twice. The changes Gallegos introduced between the first and second editions indicate that in each case the connection between theme on the one hand, and the plot and characters on the other, became closer. However rapidly the first draft of the novel was produced, the work as we now know it is not the outcome of "spontaneous" technique. It reveals with great clarity Gallegos' resolve to knit together as firmly as possible his theme and the narrative which expresses it. This is, of course, usually the case with a good novel of ideas. *Doña Perfecta* is another characteristic example. There are novels of ideas written "arborescently", that is, with the narrative growing freely and naturally out of the ideological conception like a tree from the earth, but in these novels there is a risk that the incidents may submerge or distort the theme. The Argentinian novelist Eduardo Mallea's *La bahía de silencio* is perhaps a case in point, and a much cruder example can be seen in the reduction of social protest to merely sporadic episodes in the Peruvian Ciro Alegría's *Los perros hambrientos*. In general when one examines such outstanding contributions to the ideological novel in Latin America as Miguel Angel Asturias' Guatemalan novel *El Señor Presidente* or the Cuban Alejo Carpentier's *Los pasos perdidos*, what can be perceived at once is the theme shaping the book both in its general structure and in its details.

Structurally, *Doña Bárbara* is a basically monolinear narrative: a single chain of incidents. The only significant divergence from this one story-line is the love-interest provided by the sequence of events which centres on Marisela. But although this sequence functions in a limited sense as a sub-plot, it is in no sense an appendage, as can be seen from an examination of the technical rôle in the novel of Marisela herself. Here three points are noteworthy. First, Marisela exists completely in her own right, independently of her relationship with Santos. This is demonstrated by the fact that she belongs to the central group of characters (Santos, Bárbara, Lorenzo, and to a subordinate degree Danger and Antonio Sandoval) who possess an abstract symbolic function as well as a concrete fictional one. She represents the *alma de la raza,* the child of *barbarie* who can be rescued by civilizing influences. Second, she is the only major female character apart from Bárbara herself, and hence the principal foil to her mother. Finally it is she who in Part III, chapter XI, by noticing the place of the bullet wound which killed Melquíades, liberates Santos from the grip of *barbarie* into which he has temporarily slipped. Marisela thus plays a triple rôle in the narrative. As a result the love-interest sequence which depends upon her reveals itself not as an attached sub-plot, but as what is, in reality, an integral part of the main plot itself.

This is a prime example of the concentration of effect which characterizes the structure of *Doña Bárbara* as a whole. The advantage of a monolinear plot, properly handled, lies precisely in this impression of compactness. But in proportion as a monolinear plot lengthens, difficulties appear. The chief of these is naturally that of maintaining sufficient variety to retain the reader's interest. Without considerable skill or inventiveness on the part of the novelist, the narrative tends to avoid monotony either by accumulating suspenseful incidents or by shifting the emphasis from one character to another; that is, it either becomes over-dramatic or it goes round corners. The multi-linear novel on the other hand avoids the problem of lack of variety very easily, owing to its various chains of incident; but in turn it runs the risk (which Dickens for example did not always avoid) of dispersing the reader's interest. It may even allow the main plot to be displaced or submerged by subordinate series of episodes. The technical interest of *Doña Bárbara*, as a narrative-structure, therefore lies in the study of the methods employed by Gallegos to maintain concentration of interest, suspense, balance and variety in this single chain of events, without overloading it. The principal feature of significance here is Gallegos' refusal to stake everything on a single dominating central character. The fact that there are two almost equally developed characters, Santos and Bárbara, in itself makes a sub-plot unnecessary, since Gallegos can turn the reader's interest at will from one to the other without losing any of the suspense. A similar though less fully developed use of this technique can be seen in the Chilean Eduardo Barrios' famous novel *El hermano asno,* with the characters of Fray Lázaro and Fray Rufino. However, it should be noted that this feature of the narrative is not fully developed in the first (1929) edition. It emerges properly only in the second (1930) edition after the changes mentioned on pp. 17-19, above.

The symmetrical contrast thus created between Santos and Bárbara projects itself onto the entire narrative, the salient feature of which is its essential dualism. Santos and Bárbara each have an acquired personality masking and repressing their inherited one. At the origin of each acquired personality is a traumatic experience. Each evolves from the first towards the second: Santos from the learned values of civilization back towards the instinctive *barbarie* of his forebears; Bárbara from her murderous hatred of the other sex, her witchcraft and avarice back towards the lost purity of her childhood. The underlying contrast is heightened by the division of the minor characters into two opposing groups: Bárbara's accomplices, Melquíades, Paiba, Apolinar, Pernalete and Danger; Santos' supporters, Antonio, Pajarote, Carmelito, Venancio, María Nieves and Mujiquita.

Even the background partakes of the dualism, being divided largely into two symbolically-named territories, Altamira (evocative of Santos' soaring vision of the future) and El Miedo (which stands for the threat represented by doña Bárbara's nefarious ideas and ways). Finally the tendency (mentioned below, p. 73) to divide the incidents into those of daylight and invigorating sunshine, and those of sinister darkness, should not be overlooked.

One of the most striking illustrations of the duality on which Gallegos bases his construction of *Doña Bárbara* is seen in the opening chapters as they now stand after the radical rearrangement in the second edition. After the scene has been set in chapter I, chapters II and III are symmetrical flash-backs establishing the characters of Santos and Bárbara with the careful parallelism mentioned above. Similarly, while one pair of chapters (IV and V) describes the arrival and decision of Santos, another pair (VI and VII) describes the reporting of his arrival to Bárbara and her reaction. Again, just as Santos' *hombría* emerges in chapter VIII (the *doma*) so Bárbara's *femininidad* and readiness for concession are emphasized in chapter IX. Finally in Part I, after the origins of the love-plot and the ideological climax have been disposed of, we perceive in chapter XIII the contrast between Bárbara the murderess of Apolinar, and Santos the saviour of Lorenzo and Marisela. Thus, with a single line of plot, elements of symmetry and contrast have appeared which create an appearance of variety and bifurcation of the narrative without in fact compromising its unity.

Distribution of Episodes

Looking at the novel as a whole, an indication of Gallegos' success in controlling his narrative is provided by comparing our impression of it with the reality. Our impression of *Doña Bárbara* is that of a novel of rapid and unflagging action. But if we return to an examination of Part I, we notice with surprise that the actual conflict has scarcely even got under way. What we have been taking for action is really only activity: movement, rapid shifts of scene. Practically nothing has really happened. Doña Bárbara has made a tentative concession and Santos has been foiled by Danger. The climax of Part I, Santos' interview with Danger and his decision to look after Lorenzo and Marisela, is basically undramatic, as if to emphasize Gallegos' refusal to rush his fences. How wise Gallegos was in this respect may be seen by comparing the pace of the Argentinian Eugenio Cambaceres' well-known realist novel *Sin rumbo,* in which the hero's evolution is severely compromised by the author's impatient desire to keep the novel hurrying along.

In Part II the rhythm quickens slightly. This is now the centre of the novel, usually the most critical part of a work of fiction: the point at which the initial creative impulse is spent, while the climax is not yet in sight. It is here that many novels flag or change course. But Gallegos is equal to the challenge. We notice that the central strand of action (the conflict) falls into two phases in Part II, with a minor division after chapter V. In the first phase Santos, who had got off to a bad start with Danger in Part I, seizes the initiative, while doña Bárbara continues the policy of concessions she had already begun. With Santos' feat at the cattle-drive in chapter IV, their stature as *llaneros* is equalized. The first phase of Part II ends with the first —and only— direct confrontation of Santos and Bárbara (chapter V). It occupies the exact centre of the novel. Subsequently the conflict becomes more open and accentuated. After this Santos *must* win. In the second phase of Part II, Paiba's counter-attack, the firing of the *llano*, is followed by Bárbara's magical machinations. It is however Marisela who reacts, not Santos, for he is being held back for his big scene in Part III. In substance it can be said that the hostilities between Santos and doña Bárbara reach a second stage of their progression, outstripping legal resorts. They pass the point of conciliation, without as yet coming finally to an outright clash.

The main structural feature of Part II is the major development of the love-interest between Santos and Marisela, which is used to separate the opening of hostilities in chapter I and the dramatic confrontation in chapter XIII. Clearly, since Part III is inevitably to be dominated by the climax of the central conflict between doña Bárbara and Santos, this is the moment to push forward his affair with Marisela and dispose of it. In fact, in Part III, while Marisela remains prominent and undergoes her principal evolution of character, only one chapter (Part III, chapter XI) is dedicated to tying up the love-affair. It is thus largely concentrated in the centre of the narrative, in order to leave room at the end.

It should not be overlooked also that if we accept in Part II a division after chapter V (i.e. practically at the centre of the novel, counting the pages, not the chapters), both here and at the end of the Part (chapter XIII) the main conflict and the love-interest cross. What in chapter V prevents Santos from reaching an accommodation with doña Bárbara is his indignation at her insinuation that he has seduced Marisela. What in chapter XIII produces Part II's major climax is the struggle of mother and daughter for Santos' love. Once more the carefully designed unity of the main conflict and the love-interest is confirmed.

Having thus successfully restrained the course of the action, Gallegos is able in Part III to quicken the tempo by giving free rein to the dramatic possibilities which have been so carefully prepared, as well as by adding a secondary sequence of events, that concerned with Paiba's murder of Carmelito and his theft of the valuable plumes. At first sight this sequence seems an adventitious and even rather crude piece of villainy. But once more a closer examination reveals the basic unity of the plot. The Paiba sequence is designed to produce a neat ending to the novel, which it does in three ways. First, it provides a convenient explanation of the death of Melquíades, which exonerates Santos. Second, it eliminates a character who would have to be got rid of anyway. Third, it enables doña Bárbara to make a final symbolic gesture by returning to Santos the funds which enable him to civilize the *llano* physically by carrying out the enclosures.

Another relevant point arising from Gallegos' revision of *Doña Bárbara* after the first edition is that, while whole chapters were transposed or re-structured, relatively little material was transferred from one chapter to another. This underlines the fact that the chapters are conceived individually as self-contained units; there is no overlapping of incidents from one to another, no blurring of their outlines. Each makes its own specific contribution to the development of the novel as a whole and has its own interior structure. This is clearly demonstrated by an examination of the chapter-endings. In almost every case we find a carefully prepared climax: a decisive event, a decision, a memorable phrase or rhetorical embellishment which rounds off the chapter and conveys an impression of completeness.

The restraint and the careful organization of the narrative are underlined by a glance at the distribution and length of the chapters. In the 1929 edition Part I had 13 chapters, Part II 10 chapters and Part III 14 chapters. In the text as we know it, on the other hand, the pattern is 13, 13 and 15, with a considerable gain in the general balance of the parts. Of the thirteen chapters of Part I, whose average length is just over six pages, nine chapters are longer than the average and four shorter. Part II is not very different. Ten chapters (including chapter I, the longest in the book) are above the average length, which is just on six pages, while three are below it. The fact that no fewer than six of Part II's thirteen chapters are of approximately equal length, compared with only three in Part I, suggests the achievement of equilibrium in the centre of the novel. In Part III, however, there is a sharp contrast. The average length of chapter drops to only four and a half pages, while in addition no fewer than nine of the fifteen chapters fall below this average length: a sure indication of much quicker tempo.

In retrospect we see that the three parts and forty-one chapters of *Doña Bárbara,* as they now stand, fall into relatively clear divisions. The exposition occupies the first five chapters of Part I, with its logical conclusion when Santos reaches his decision not to sell Altamira. It fulfils admirably its triple function of grasping the reader's interest, introducing the major characters and conveying the information needed to understand the circumstances of the narrative. Dramatic suspense is present from the opening chapter. The parallel between Santos and doña Bárbara is firmly established in chapters II and III, and Santos' resolution thereafter forms a natural climax. The rest of Part I may be regarded as the novel's first development. It begins appropriately with the news of Santos' arrival reaching Bárbara and, apart from preparing the love plot in chapter XI, contains the novel's ideological climax (chapter X). In general in this section of the narrative Santos' fortunes fall, and he is specifically defeated by Danger in the last chapter.

Part II, as we have seen, begins in splendid contrast with Santos' recovery of the initiative. Once more there is a division after chapter V, the main interview between Santos and Bárbara, which is the novel's centre of balance. Now that it is established that Santos is not amenable to Bárbara's attractions, the first phase of conciliation and compromise on her part comes to an end. Henceforth she remains absent from the narrative for no fewer than seven chapters, which are largely devoted to Santos and Marisela. Only at the end does she reappear with sinister dramatic force, to provide a splendid curtain scene to Part II, the second act of the drama. The seven chapters during which she is off-stage form an interesting, and relatively less dramatic, semi-interlude in Part II, and constitute, in relation to the dramatic structure of the novel as a whole, a kind of pause before the fireworks of Part III.

Part III itself shows events coming rapidly to a head after the vicissitudes in Santos' fortunes which are proper to the middle of the novel. G. L. Kolb, in the only article which deals seriously with the structure of *Doña Bárbara,* notes the way in which this Part is skilfully arranged, almost like a series of concentric circles. These express the idea which dominates this section of the narrative, that "las cosas vuelven al lugar de donde salieron". In each case —Melquíades and Cabos Negros (the opening symbolic episode), Marisela and her father, Santos, Paiba, Danger and doña Bárbara— there is an implicit circularity, a return to source, which gives an impression "redondez" to the conclusion of the novel. Actually Part III can be seen falling into three parts. Chapters I to III inclusive contain, after the symbolic opening, a downward spiral of events (the demoralisation and flight of Marisela, the failure of the *queseras* and the murder of Carmelito and his brother) which leads to Santos' sombre decision, the major turning-point of his character. This decision in turn produces the central development of Part III, the peak of the action, involving Santos' attack on the Mondragones, the condemnation, flight and death of Paiba, and, most dramatic of all, the duel between Santos and Melquíades. This sequence may be said to reach a double climax in chapters X and XI. In the former the return of Melquíades' body, Bárbara's reaction, and the death of Paiba neatly round off the events of the sequence. In the latter —the emotional climax of the novel— Santos and Marisela find each other fully at last and their evolution ends. The last four chapters are concentrated on doña Bárbara herself and constitute a prolonged epilogue with its own dramatic climax in chapter XIV.

Doña Bárbara is, whatever its other shortcomings, unquestionably Gallegos' most carefully constructed work of fiction. His two successive radical revisions of the text produced in the end a taut, symmetrical, supremely dramatic narrative. There can be little doubt that a great deal of the book's enormous impact derives from

the fact that it is one of the few Latin-American examples of the
well-made novel.[11]

Narrative Technique

Gallegos' success in lending to *Doña Bárbara* the appearance of
a novel which unfolds at a consistently rapid pace —ingeniously
deceptive as this appearance sometimes is prior to Part III— is
unquestionably one of the keys to the book's striking success with
the reading public. It is principally achieved by his systematic use of
scene and his relative avoidance both of summary and of extensive
description. Gallegos' concern is to maintain in the reader the illusion
of being shown the events while they are happening, with a minimum
of flash-backs and reported incidents. This creates in the reader's
mind the impression of being present at the scene of the action and
hence of being involved in a forward-moving time-sequence which,
in spite of the tenses of the verbs, is accepted as in a sense current
time. Once this impression has been created, and suspense has been
built up through the reader's identification with the situations, it is
essential to avoid disturbing the effect by halting the time-flow, or by
inverting it, in order to describe previous events. This is one of the
main differences between the dramatic novel and, for example, the
psychological novel. There the alternation of current and past time,
or the slowing down of the novel's inner time-sequence to allow for
long trains of reflections or descriptions of states of mind, is relatively
unimportant. A comparison of the treatment of time in *Doña*

[11]Not all critics are agreed on this point. Ricardo Baeza, reviewing *Doña
Bárbara* in *El Sol* (Madrid, 14 January 1930), M. P. González, 'A propósito de
Doña Bárbara', *Bulletin of Spanish Studies* 7 (1930) 162-167, and J. R. Spell
in his chapter on Gallegos in *Contemporary Spanish American Fiction* (Chapel
Hill, 1944) 205-238, all agree. E. Rodríguez Monegal, however, in *Narradores
de esta América* (Montevideo 1963) p. 58, after enumerating the main contents
of the novel, writes: "Todos estos elementos están en la novela. Pero no se
integran en un cuadro homogéneo y coherente. El recurso narrativo de
Gallegos es hilvanarlos, uno tras otro, esperando que acaben por soldarse. Y
se sueldan. Pero siguen sin integrar la unidad."

Bárbara and for example in Eduardo Mallea's study of a woman's problem of loneliness, *Todo verdor perecerá,* illustrates the point very clearly.[12]

An important contributory factor is the very brief time-span into which the novel is compressed. The events of Part I, for example, occupy less than a fortnight. Part II, though deliberately sparing in time-notations, begins about a fortnight before the *Jueves Santo* mentioned in the sixth chapter, and reaches the end of the rainy season. Part III again covers about a fortnight or three weeks. Thus we have the impression of a day-by-day account of events as they occur. Flash-backs, in Part I, where they are most useful, are restricted to chapters II, III and the beginning of XIII for the unavoidable purpose of conveying information about major characters. Elsewhere, prior events are reported mainly in conversation: Santos' reference to Lorenzo's life in Caracas, Mujiquita's evocation of his companionship with Santos at the University, Carmelito's description of the murder of his parents. Only very rarely does Gallegos forsake this method, when for example Santos recalls first hearing Melquíades' voice. Otherwise practically nothing happens that the reader does not appear to see happening. So consistent is this technique that Gallegos is able to take cunning advantage of it in Part III, chapter VI. There, for the only significant time in the narrative, we learn from Antonio that Santos has defied Danger to shoot it out, and that he has been rounding up cattle on Bárbara's ground without her permission. Clearly, to have presented either of these actions as scenes where the reader was a direct spectator, would have involved the risk of overstressing Santos' relapse from his earlier principles. Relying therefore on the impressions created by his scenic technique, Gallegos slips this information in to reinforce Santos' decline, without really harming his image.

[12]See the preface to my edition of this novel, Oxford, Pergamon, 1968, esp. p. xxiii.

Similarly, descriptions are rarely allowed to interfere with the reader's impression of rapid narrative rhythm. Where they refer to physical appearances or states of mind they are normally brief and are immediately followed by a return to direct scene-presentation. Otherwise they are descriptions of action and dramatic movement: the *rodeo,* the *vaquería,* the crocodile hunt: animated descriptions which, without necessarily thrusting the story onwards, are never static. Many of them illustrate Gallegos' effective use of *costumbrista* elements. *Costumbrismo* differs from realism in that, while both terms connote observation of external reality, the *costumbrista* writer is essentially concerned to record and preserve the more picturesque aspects of the traditional ways of life and usages of a given locality, rather than trying to present an objective picture. *Doña Bárbara,* which takes place against the background of a disappearing pattern of life on the *llano,* contains plenty of *costumbrismo;* but never simply for its own sake. Each *cuadro* is functionally related to the development of the novel as a whole. The *peones'* superstitious discussion of El Cotizudo is engineered by Pajarote to further Santos' character in action; the taming of La Catira is designed to reflect that of Marisela; the rustic dance at Altamira, with its charming *coplas,* precipitates a crisis in the relationship of Santos and Marisela; finally the descriptions of the crocodile hunt and Melquíades' failure with Cabos Negros portend the future collapse of doña Bárbara's faction. In each case the intrinsic *costumbrista* interest is only part of the reason for the episode's inclusion in the novel; it is also there to serve a specific technical purpose.

A final feature which contributes to the vivacity of the narrative is Gallegos' reliance on dialogue. It constitutes more than thirty per cent of the text, a fact which strikingly emphasises Bárbara's own grimly impressive laconism.

Dialogue also affords Gallegos a useful means of bringing in commentary. This is perhaps most notable in the case of the long dialogue between Santos and Lorenzo in Part I, chapter X, which is simply a device for explaining Gallegos' own ideas. In practically all novels the selection and arrangement of the episodes themselves tells the reader something about the author's outlook. But few novelists are content with just this. They want to add a moral, social or psychological commentary on what is happening, which will bring out its implications more fully. In fact this is one of the features which distinguish genuinely literary fiction from the novel of mere entertainment.

D. G. Castanien analyses Gallegos' methods of conveying psychological commentary in the work. What emerges is his heavy reliance on the traditional manner. Statements on the part of the author, made from the standpoint of omniscience, are found along with direct reports of the character's thoughts introduced by a verb like "se dijo" or "pensaba", and with indirect interior monologue, that is, paraphrases or summaries of the character's thoughts supplied by the author using the third person. Particularly prominent are chapters X and XI of Part II in which Marisela and Santos reflect on their respective emotional situations, and the interview between doña Bárbara and Paiba in Part III, chapter IV. In the first the dialogue of Marisela and Genoveva gives way imperceptibly to an imaginary dialogue between Marisela and Santos which takes place in the former's mind, followed by the clumsy remark: "esto no sucedió sino en la imaginación de Marisela" (294). In the second, Santos' thoughts slip gradually into indirect monologue: " ¿Está en la cocina, preparándole la comida como a él le agrada? " (300) and then suddenly back into the direct form: "Vas a salir y tienes que hacerte a un lado . . ." (300) in a curious combination of methods. Finally in the third, the dialogue of Bárbara and Paiba is parallelled at intervals by their very different real thoughts. All this is quite acceptable, if a trifle unsophisticated, even by the standards of the novel in Gallegos' own day. What does give the technique a rather dated appearance is the frequency and obtrusiveness of Gallegos' appearances as the omniscient narrator. While what is sometimes called "the disappearance of the author" in modern fiction remains an invention on the part of critics, we are entitled to expect a greater degree of disguise than Gallegos bothers to use. In particular his moral judgements on the less agreeable characters and his explanation of motives in his own voice, rather than by a greater use of discreet interior monologue, reveal an over-anxious reluctance to let the novel speak for itself. Gallegos' habit of making his characters undergo sudden climactic experiences which radically alter their personalities (cf. Marisela after her bath: "Ella misma es otra persona" [I, ix, 156]; doña Bárbara after her dialogue with Santos: "Ya tú no eres la misma" [II, v, 253]; and Santos Luzardo after his resort to violence: "convertido en otro hombre" [III, v, 375]) also seems curiously antiquated.

Chapter III

Doña Bárbara

While critical reaction to *Doña Bárbara*, considered as a narrative, has generally been favourable though unanalytic, the same cannot be said of doña Bárbara herself as a fictional character. From a very early stage, indeed, critics have disagreed about her worth as a fictional creation, about the credibility of her development and about the meaning and symbolism that are to be attributed to her. Thus Ciro Alegría, himself a novelist of distinction, asserts that "doña Bárbara es un personaje con una clara motivación que fracasa por exceso de tesis". M. Morínigo voices a general criticism, also accepted by Waldo Ross, that Bárbara, in common with other characters of Gallegos, is externally motivated and lacks the interior life of a real person. Jorge Mañach and Concha Meléndez regard her on the contrary as "un admirable estudio de psicología", a view which is shared by Torres Rioseco and Damboriena.[13]

A second divergence concerns the ending and doña Bárbara's apparent change of character in Part III, chapter XIV ('La estrella en la mira'). This was already strongly criticized by Rafael Angarita Arvelo in *Historia y crítica de la novela en Venezuela* (Berlin, 1938), by Lowell Dunham in his excellent book and most recently by Cyril Jones. Finally, while doña Bárbara has been seen traditionally as personifying in different ways the *latifundista* class, the *llano*

[13]See C. Alegría, 'Notas sobre Rómulo Gallegos' in *La novela iberoamericana* (ed. A. Torres Rioseco), Albuquerque, 1951, p. 52; M. Morínigo, 'Civilización y barbarie en *Facundo y Doña Bárbara*', *Revista Nacional de Cultura* (Caracas), 161 (1963), p. 106; W. Ross, 'La soledad en la obra de Rómulo Gallegos', *ib.*, 148/9 (1961), p. 36; F. Massiani, *El hombre y la naturaleza venezolana en Rómulo Gallegos,* Caracas, 1965, p. 95, where the views of Mañach and Meléndez are reported; A. Torres Rioseco, *Novelistas contemporáneos de América,* Santiago, 1939, p. 100 and A. Damboriena, *Rómulo Gallegos y la problemática venezolana,* Caracas, 1960, p. 336.

itself and the *alma de la raza* of Venezuela, a more recent development
has tended to emphasize the purely mythical element in her character.
This is already a feature of Liscano's approach to doña Bárbara when
he admirably synthesizes the position as follows:—

> Doña Bárbara existe y "es" en tres planos: el primero, de índole
> personal, se refiere al cruel sacrificio lujurioso del cual fue objeto,
> a su desviación consiguiente, a su existencia de mujerona frustrada
> y codiciosa, a sus malas artes, a su pasión final por Santos Luzardo
> [the personal plane]; el segundo la tipifica en función venezolana
> como representación de una vida salvaje y feudal, como personifi-
> cación de la llanura [the symbolic plane]; . . . el tercero la
> identifica como un arquetipo. la Fémina primordial . . .
> emparentada con Kali y Lamia, con Lilith y Coatlicue, todas
> ellas figuraciones de la Gran Madre procreadora de vida y de
> muerte, de la Gran Prostituta, oscura divinidad de los tiempos
> [the mythical plane]. Doña Bárbara la dañera, la Devoradora de
> Hombres, la cruel Esfinge de la Sabana, está visiblemente en el
> umbral de un mito milenario (p. 104).

A similar approach is visible in Chapman's interesting essay and
comes to a climax in Michalski's article in *PMLA*, 1969, in which
only the mythical interpretation of doña Bárbara is really accepted.
In total contrast Massiani (see note 12) long ago asserted "hay tal
abundancia de reacciones y mudanzas en el alma de los personajes . . .
que el procedimiento simbólico pasa a ser completamente subalterno
y accidental" (p. 89). A brief reconsideration of Bárbara's character
may help to resolve some of the disagreement.

The first question which must be asked about a major fictional
character is whether that character evolves. Here there can be no
question. Bárbara undergoes a very marked change of outlook in
the course of the narrative, underlined by the comment of her
conscience at the end of Part II, chapter V: "Ya tú no eres la misma"
(253). At the end of the book she is quite clearly a different woman
from the "mujer terrible" of chapter I who "tiene su cementerio".
This in itself surely disposes of Alegría's view that Bárbara, like
Santos, is a character "hecho de una sola pieza". A feature of both,
on the contrary, as we have seen, is their dualism.

Santos is an attractive, well-intentioned, rational figure with a potentiality for impulsiveness and violence; Bárbara is an evil woman whom Gallegos does not hesitate to call "repugnante" (II, iii, 219), a murderess, an unnatural mother, but nevertheless a woman possessed not only of a certain grandeur, but also of a repressed capacity for "sentimiento puro" which is emphasized in Part I, chapter III, at the very beginning of the reader's acquaintance with her. This simple, indeed over-simplified, contrast between the divergent aspects of her personality is the very essence of her character and to that extent justifies the criticism that she lacks convincing interior life. On the other hand it must be recognized that this is a novel dominated by theme expressed in terms of a rather fast-moving plot. In such a case the exploration of character in depth which can be undertaken in a slow-moving psychological novel such as the Argentinian Eduardo Mallea's *Todo verdor perecerá* or the Chilean Eduardo Barrios' *El hermano asno* is ruled out. The Cuban Alejo Carpentier's *Los pasos perdidos,* whose theme is similar to that of *Doña Bárbara* though in reverse, is a fair comparison. Few critics would suggest that the psychological presentation of its characters —who, like those of Gallegos here, are representative and even symbolic— is more convincingly achieved. The limitations are similar in both cases.

The first stage of Bárbara's character, her establishment as a fictional figure, occurs in the first three chapters. It is of course negative. The conversation between Santos and the *bonguero* conveys the image of a figure at once fierce ("mujer terrible"), cunningly sinister ("faculta en brujerías"), and murderous ("tiene su cementerio"). In chapter II we are introduced to part of her symbolism: she is "criatura y personificación de los tiempos que corrían" (55); the reference is to Venezuela under the despotic rule of Juan Vicente Gómez. Finally we are offered two pointers to the origin of her evil personality. One, in true naturalist manner, is associated with her heredity: she is a *mestiza,* combining the violence of her white father with the sombre sensuality of her Indian mother. The other is the traumatic experience of her rape. The rest of chapter III accumulates further negative features: her cruel lack of maternal instinct, her avarice, her murder of Apolinar (who, in the 1929 edition, was her husband), and her grossly superstitious dealings with *El Socio.*

But Gallegos already introduces attenuating details. For one thing, we are not sure whether all this is truth or hearsay: "Eso es lo que cuenta la gente" says the *bonguero,* and "Eso contaban" Gallegos adds in chapter II. Secondly he reemphasizes her uncorrupted reserve of "sentimiento puro" by the reference to "una pequeña cosa pura" at the end of chapter III, leading to the hint immediately after that she is capable of redemption by love. Thirdly, by associating her with the *llano* itself, which we know he saw ambivalently, Gallegos invests her implicitly with some of its positive qualities. As E. A. Johnson notes, doña Bárbara and the *llano* are only *semibárbaras* really. The qualities of tragic grandeur and beauty which Bárbara shares with the *llano* are further emphasized by the way in which Gallegos also associates Bárbara with two of its birds: the lovely but ill-fated *gaván* and the noble and stately though predatory *gavilán.*

When in chapter VI Bárbara actually appears on stage it is with El Brujeador and Paiba. The former she respects, the latter she despises. Here Gallegos has implicitly established a scale of evil in which she is not at the bottom. Her language, too, terse, mordant and expressive, sparingly used and never vulgar or incorrect, expresses her commanding personality. In spite of all her negative qualities, by chapter VII we share Carmelito's grudging admiration for her.

The start of Bárbara's evolution occurs in chapter IX with her return to feminine clothes. This change in her appearance portends her eventual moral change, leading to her discovery at the end of the novel of something of the girl described in the flash-back which has survived in the "mujer terrible". It is deftly accompanied by comments on her "superioridad" and "dominio sobre los demás" (131). Henceforth her character undulates according to the exigencies of the narrative, with the emphasis resting at times on her "malos instintos" (II, iii, 216) and at times on her "sentimientos nuevos" (II, v, 244). Gallegos now met one of the technical problems inherent in the book once its theme had taken shape: that of keeping doña Bárbara at the level of her reputation, presenting her as an adversary fully worthy of crossing swords with Santos, but at the same time making her fail all along the line. It is questionable whether Gallegos solves this problem adequately. The fact is that apart from attempting without success to fascinate Santos both directly and through magic, and later sending Melquíades out to bring him back alive or dead, Bárbara simply surrenders the initiative to her opponent. The real doña Bárbara, one feels, "mujer de pelo en pecho", would have taken more active measures. How does Gallegos explain her failure to do so? First (Part II, chapter I) by asserting that luck, hitherto on her side, now deserted her. Second, by suggesting three times in succession that in some mysterious way Santos presented her with a totally new situation with which she was unable to cope (see the references in this chapter to "algo nuevo" [189], to the fact that "por primera vez" she felt respect for a male [204], and finally [II, iv, 230] to her life's taking "un rumbo imprevisto"). The first of these two explanations, which involves the wholly unexpected corollary (added in the second edition) that Bárbara was "incapaz de concebir un verdadero plan" (188) is simply unconvincing. The second, which leads to the bald statement that "sus sentimientos habituales la abandonaron de pronto" (230) without her being able to recognize what took their place, is vague.

Part II, chapter V ('Las mudanzas de doña Bárbara'), which now follows, is the key chapter for her development. Here Gallegos faces squarely the task of portraying the struggle of Bárbara with herself, and her sudden discovery under the influence of her "ansia insaciada de una verdadera pasión" (245) of "aquella región desconocida de su alma" full of "sentimientos, nuevos en su vida" and "ansia de bien" (i.e. the lost purity of her girlhood), which at the end of the book will triumph over her "instintos rapaces". In the centre of the narrative, just before leaving the stage for seven consecutive chapters, she meets her moment of truth and emerges with the message of her conscience: "Ya tú no eres la misma" (253).

When she reappears at the end of Part II the conflict is still unresolved. Gallegos refers twice in chapter XIII to her continuing duality: "El hábito del mal y el ansia del bien, lo que ella era y lo que anhelaba ser" (324), "Las dos porciones del alma desdoblada" (327). In Part III the oscillation of her character is most visible. At one extreme (chapter IV), now wholly in the grip of passion, she is ready to shed her past completely and give free rein to her "ansia de renovación". "A todo esto estaba dispuesta: a entregar sus obras y a cambiar de vida . . . Seré otra mujer — decíase una y otra vez" (369). But after her rebuff by Santos the memory of her previous murders (specifically referred to in the plural, III, vii, 394) recurs, and her character touches its lowest point with her decision to send Melquíades to meet Santos in Rincón Hondo.

Chiefly, however, what Gallegos repeatedly emphasizes (in preparation for the penultimate chapter) is her indecision and irresolution: "La confusión de sentimientos que reinaba en su espíritu" (III, i, 338), her "sentimientos contradictorios" (III, x, 416), and in chapter VII itself, at the very moment of sending Melquíades on his sinister mission, her inability to clarify her own motives. Santos' appearance with the corpse of El Brujeador tips the balance: Bárbara capitulates. But Gallegos is too wise to waste the effect he has prepared. Her capitulation is divided into two parts. In the first (chapters X and XII) Bárbara sets to rights the material and moral wrong she has done to Santos, returning his plumes and explaining away the death of Melquíades. Now, at the beginning of chapter XIII, her character is subtly refurbished morally by a change in her legend: from having been a "ser siniestro" in the popular mind, she now emerges as a "heroina", "fascinadora", almost a "personaje de leyenda" worthy of "íntima devoción" (436). After a final flare-up of jealousy, noble feeling associated with the memory of her own first love triumphs and doña Bárbara makes her supreme act of sacrifice.

What are we to conclude? Certainly in view of the careful preparation, stage by stage, for the triumph of Bárbara's repressed "sentimiento puro", first referred to as early as Part I, chapter III, we cannot accept the statement by Jones that "there is very little hint of explanation of her ultimate magnanimity". Still less acceptable is his assertion that the ending of the novel represents "a monstrous betrayal" of Gallegos' technical skill. But the dissatisfaction of Jones and others with the ending, though due in part to their hasty evaluation of Bárbara's character, does probably indicate that Gallegos' technique was not fully equal to the task of portraying Bárbara's psychology with entire conviction. Perhaps, as Sturgis E. Leavitt suggests in 'Sex versus Symbolism in *Doña Bárbara*', *Revista de Estudios Hispánicos* (Alabama) I (1967), 117-120, that task itself was an impossible one. My own view is that Gallegos was unwise to avoid an emotional encounter between Bárbara and Santos. Leavitt argues that for Santos to have rebuffed her physically would have made him appear to Latin-American readers as lacking in *machismo*. I doubt this, given Gallegos' fictional ability. As it is, Santos' evolution is based on incidents and thus carries more conviction. But the gradual emergence and final predominance of Bárbara's repressed better self is not produced by actual happenings. It is an internal psychological process. This Gallegos was not quite adequately equipped to portray. The successful psychological novel is one of the rarer categories of Latin-American fiction.

Another approach to doña Bárbara remains to be mentioned briefly. The joint desire to explain away deficiencies in Gallegos' portrayal of her character from a realist standpoint, and to associate Venezuela's major novelist with the current fashion for "realismo mágico", has led some critics to attempt an interpretation of Bárbara which leans heavily on her "mythical" qualities. "Doña Bárbara es sólo medio humana", writes Michalski, "su otra mitad es a la vez animal y sobrenatural . . . es la Belle Dame sans Merci serrana o selvática de las leyendas y cuentos folklóricos". He goes on to identify her with the *vouivres* of French folklore and the *chamas* of the Venezuelan indians, just as Liscano does with Kali, Lamia and other mythical figures of evil.

Two objections are possible. The first is that such an interpretation does not appear to have been part of Gallegos' intentions. In his well-known Havana lecture on the text, reproduced in *Una posición en la vida* (see note 3), Gallegos stated explicitly: "en la gestación de mis obras no parto de la concepción del símbolo —como si dijéramos en el aire— para desembocar en la imaginación del personaje que pueda realizarlo; sino que el impulso creador me viene siempre del hallazgo del personaje ya significativo, dentro de la realidad circundante" (p. 404). Speaking directly about doña Bárbara he declared: "¿Símbolo? Sí. De cuanto entonces era predominio de barbarie y de la violencia en mi país." Gallegos, that is, places the emphasis on reality, not myth, as the origin of doña Bárbara, and restricts her symbolism to that which is emphasized in the novel itself, related to "los tiempos que corrían" in Venezuela.

But writers are notoriously unreliable when attempting to explain their own work. Perhaps Gallegos was unaware of the implications of his own creation. Even so a second objection remains. Michalski's article is persuasive, never more so than when he uses his theory to account convincingly for Bárbara's curious passivity in the face of the threat posed by Santos, and in his explanation of the snake symbol in the last chapter. But if we accept his interpretation as a whole, what is the result? It is that we can no longer take *Doña Bárbara* seriously as a novel of ideas. Yet whatever shortcomings we may discover in the ideas expressed in this novel, there is no doubt that this is what Gallegos set out to write. Only in so far as a mythical interpretation can be harmonized with the obvious ideological intention of the book, can it be accepted. Bárbara stands or falls as a character, a woman, at most as a symbol of Venezuelan barbarism, not as a fairy-tale witch or a goddess of evil.

Santos Luzardo

Gallegos' portrayal of Santos Luzardo has, in general, been more kindly treated by critics than that of Bárbara. Pedro Díaz Seijas in *Rómulo Gallegos, realidad y símbolo,* Caracas, 1965, p. 56, praises Santos' "riqueza psicológica". Damboriena, in a long analysis, considers that he stands out beyond all Gallegos' other male protagonists. J. Rivas Rivas and O. Araujo both emphasize his *voluntarismo,* while E. A. Johnson stresses his evolution from rationalism to emotion. Finally Lucila de Pérez Díaz[14] makes the valid point that Santos holds his place of honour among Gallegos' heroes chiefly because he most of all succeeds in overcoming that juvenile *machismo* which is so integral a part of Latin-American barbarism. Only timidly has it been suggested that Santos is a trifle over-idealized. What seems to have escaped comment so far is the effect which Gallegos' divided outlook about the *barbarie* of Venezuela had on his presentation of Santos. Also noteworthy are some of the modifications to Santos' character which Gallegos introduced between the first and second editions of *Doña Bárbara.*

A misleading factor is a tendency to see Santos as a figure of contrast to doña Bárbara rather than as an independent figure in his

[14]L. de Pérez Díaz, 'Evolución progresiva de un protagonista de Rómulo Gallegos', *Revista Nacional de Cultura,* 53 (1945), 13-22.

own right. This tendency is natural enough. In many respects Santos and doña Bárbara *are* inseparable. Bárbara, as her name implies, represents *barbarie*; Santos represents civilization. M. A. Martínez develops the point that this contrast between the two characters is extended even to the light imagery associated with them in the novel.[15] Doña Bárbara and her designs are presented predominantly in terms of darkness, with an accumulation of words such as *tenebroso*, *sombrío*, *oscuro* and their cognates. Her first appearance and other later ones are at night, as befits her evil *brujerías*. Santos, on the other hand, first appears in the light of the midday sun, his activities are principally conducted in the light of day, and light imagery and symbolism are consistently used in connection with the positive, optimistic aspect of the story. But a comparison of the duality visible in both Bárbara and Santos reveals Gallegos' divergence from such a simple pattern of contrast. Of Bárbara Johnson writes: "It would seem that Gallegos is such an optimist about human nature that his personification of barbarity really has deep within her . . . a genuine 'ansia de bien'." This is quite true, as we see from Gallegos' identification of her with the *llanura*: "recia y brava" but with somewhere inside her a "región incontaminada" (II, v, 251). Is Santos simply the exact opposite?

At first sight he is, though from the outset his duality is more pronounced than hers. The first comment on his personality refers to "sentimientos contrarios", followed by a reference to his alternate "entusiasmo" and "desaliento". His vivacious questioning of the *bonguero* gives way suddenly to "mutismo sombrío". The alert reader at once perceives that this ambivalence is the root of his character, while his attractive appearance, his intelligence, and the courage shown in his confrontation with Melquíades at the *palodeagua*, are merely the conventional outer trappings of the fictional hero.

[15]M. A. Martínez, 'Las noches en El Miedo', *Revista Nacional de Cultura*, 127 (1958), 43-57.

Even before it is explained, his ambivalence has been translated into terms of plot. Unlike Bárbara's duality, which condemns her to relative passivity in the face of the threat posed by Santos, his sets the whole action going by producing the sudden change of intentions in chapter I.

In chapter II the origin of Santos' personality-conflict is explained, like Bárbara's, in terms partly of heredity, partly of a traumatic experience: the murder of his brother by his father, followed by his father's death. This explosion of violence, followed by the brusque removal from the *llano* to the city, produces a marked change in Santos, who, formerly "fino y reflexivo", becomes "obtuso y abúlico". His faculties lie fallow while he digests his terrible experience. When he recovers himself the instinctive responses inherited from his *llanero* forebears and fomented by his boyhood have been repressed. A passage in the first edition, later removed, suggests that this repression was conscious and deliberate:

> Pero al emprender los estudios de jurisprudencia no lo guió, propiamente, una inclinación intelectual. Espíritu complejo, doblado de razonador e impulsivo, lo predominante en él era la tendencia a la acción y si escogió una carrera científica no fue por obedecer a una verdadera vocación, sino porque el estudio era un ejercicio de la voluntad, una disciplina, y la que con mayor eficacia podía reprimir las tendencias hacia la vida libre y bárbara del instinto. Lo interesante no era llegar a ser abogado, sino ser estudiante y de la ciencia quizás más hostil a todo lo que fuese inclinación natural de su espíritu: lo interesante era sofocar al bárbaro que alentaba en él, depurarse de toda tendencia impulsiva (*Doña Bárbara*, 1st ed., 1929, 29).

Now, however, the meeting with Melquíades releases Santos' buried *acometividad*. In the foreground of the rest of the story is its struggle to overcome his acquired characteristics of reason and self-control. In fact, in the 1929 edition, Santos' struggle with himself, seen in rather crude terms, was more prominent than at present, relative to his struggle with Bárbara. In the revision of 1929-30 Gallegos altered the emphasis slightly to bring the struggle with

Bárbara —who is now subtly ennobled— more into balance with
Santos' inner conflict. At the same time that conflict itself became
modified. Santos' original *barbarie*, nearer to the surface and
presented in terms of *odio* and *animalidad*, turns into what it is now
—something closer to *hombría*.

Meanwhile Santos faces the external struggle, with the *llano* and
with doña Bárbara. On this plane of the narrative his salient
characteristic is energy, the will and capacity to act. But in which
direction? Ideally, Santos means his actions to be positive, to be
directed to "la obra patriótica, la lucha contra el mal imperante"
(I, v, 91). But already Gallegos stresses their negative potentiality
also: the danger that they may express on the contrary the "bárbaras
tendencias" which now seem on the point of release. So far the
parallel with doña Bárbara is complete, even down to the reference
in chapter V to "dos corrientes contrarias" in Santos corresponding
to the famous image of the two rivers which Gallegos uses to
illustrate Bárbara's duality in chapter IV.

In the first phase of development of Santos' character, in which
his positive ideals prevail and give rise to appropriate action, we may
agree with Rivas Rivas that three successive stages are clearly defined:
the taming of Paiba, the taming of the horse and ultimately the
taming of Bárbara and the *llano* which she personifies. The taming
of Marisela occupies an intermediate position. It is related both to
the second stage, through the symbol of La Catira, and to the final
stage, since the taming of both Bárbara and her daughter are completed
simultaneously. The order of the first two stages is of great
importance. It confirms the fact that Gallegos saw the problem in
human rather than socio-economic terms. Like Ganivet, whom he
read, he saw the need to "obrar sobre el espíritu de los hombres" as
the first task. It was the error of the Spanish *regeneracionistas*
repeating itself, as it did elsewhere in Latin America.

By the end of chapter VIII Santos has overcome his first obstacle,

the distrust of his *peones,* brushed aside Paiba, and passed his first
test of *hombría* by taming the stallion. The meeting with Lorenzo
Barquero highlights his *energía* and *voluntad* in contrast to the latter's
abulia. At the same time an element of feeling has appeared alongside his activity and intelligence: compassion for Lorenzo and for
Marisela, the latter already —significantly— converted into "compasión
diferente" when her physical beauty appears from beneath the grime.
Again this emotion is swiftly translated into action when at the end
of Part I, with a characteristic "fogosa decisión" which reveals his
repressed impulsiveness, he snatches Lorenzo and Marisela from the
grasp of Mr Danger.

Here we notice a further aspect which may have symbolic value.
As well as standing in general for civilized qualities (law, order,
reason, progress and enlightenment), Santos now appears as the
particular symbol of Venezuela's younger generation of intellectual
dirigentes, stepping in where the previous generation (symbolized by
Lorenzo) had failed, and saving the country's future (Marisela) from
foreign domination and corruption.

At the beginning of Part II, in a chapter added in 1930 during the
revision of the first edition, Santos, having refused to meet violence
with violence, nevertheless brilliantly recovers the initiative which he
had lost in his earlier interview with Danger. By a striking combination
of intelligence and legal finesse he traps Danger and turns the tables
on Bárbara in a completely non-violent manoeuvre.

Chapters IV and V of Part II contain, as we have seen, the centre
of balance of the whole novel. Here the equilibrium between the
opposing forces is abandoned. Doña Bárbara for the first time "da
su brazo a torcer" and begins consciously to accept subjugation by
Santos' personality. In turn his personality here reaches its peak of
idealization as he is seen, through her eyes, adorned with every
attractive quality:

aquel insólito aspecto varonil, aquella mezcla de dignidad y de

delicadeza, aquella impresión de fortaleza y de dominio de sí
mismo que trascendía del fuego reposado de las miradas del
joven, de sus ademanes justos, de sus palabras netamente pronun-
ciadas . . . (II, iv, 230).

For the rest of Part II Santos remains at this level: self-controlled,
"enemigo de las represalias" (II, viii, 268), peacefully determined to
"acabar con ciertas costumbres del llano" (II, ix, 278), and even —as
yet— completely disinterested in his feelings about Marisela, which
he is able to analyse with "fría imparcialidad" (II, xi, 296). Gallegos
is clearly preparing the ground for Santos' sudden change in Part III.
Meanwhile the action proceeds unhurriedly, as Gallegos reserves the
climax of the conflict for Part III and seizes the opportunity to
develop the love-interest. Logically, since Santos is already feeling
the call of the *llano*, to which he is soon in some measure to surrender,
he ought to feel the attraction of Bárbara who personifies it. But
here Gallegos refuses to follow the symbolism through to the end.
Santos feels no more than "curiosidad, meramente intelectual"
(II, iv, 234) about Bárbara, suddenly replaced by an intimate
repulsion. Nor is this because of Marisela, whom five chapters later
he is still able to see as a possible obstacle to his personal plans.
Santos is just not tempted by Bárbara's charms. How much more
interesting the novel would have been, and how much more convincing
Santos' character if he had been, however briefly!

The crisis of Santos' development arrives in Part II, chapter XII,
announced by the reawakening of his dormant *llanero* instincts at
the *doma* and the *vaquería general.* Suddenly in the midst of the
cattle-taming he feels his acquired values slip away. *Barbarie* ceases
to be evil and becomes beautiful, even the source of a fresh pattern
of vital values:

> Santos Luzardo compartió con los peones los peligros de aquellos
> choques, y las emociones lo hicieron olvidarse otra vez de los
> proyectos civilizadores. Bien estaba la llanura, así, ruda y bravía.
> Era la barbarie; mas . . . la barbarie tiene sus encantos, es algo
> hermoso que vale la pena vivirlo, es la plenitud del hombre . . . (310).

Here Santos' evolution breaks away completely from being a mirror image of Bárbara's, reflecting it in reverse. Nothing in her development really parallels Santos' change here. Gallegos' ambivalence with regard to *barbarie*, discussed earlier (pp. 12-13) has caught up with his fictional hero. All that is now needed is an event which will trigger off the resort to action of Santos' hitherto repressed personality, now unexpectedly back in control. That event is the murder of Carmelito and his brother. Denied justice by Pernalete, Santos at length decides to meet force with force: ironically, at the very moment when Bárbara is ready to lay down her arms. But with this difference: Santos' violence is short-lived and exercised only against wrong-doers: the Mondragones, Danger, doña Bárbara and Melquíades. Even so Gallegos attenuates it. Only once do we see Santos really "convertido en otro hombre fiero y sombrío" (III, v, 375): when he attacks the Mondragones. His illegal fencing-in of Corozalito and his raids into Bárbara's land are not shown as scenes in the narrative, but are merely mentioned by Antonio (III, vi, 388). Finally he shoots Melquíades only in intention. Long before then he has begun to feel remorse for his potential "catástrofe espiritual" (III, v, 376) and fear of "una intempestiva regresión a la barbarie" (III, viii, 401). We note however that the verb-forms "a lo que *pudieran* inducirlo" and "todo cuanto *desaparecería*" indicate that the moral collapse has not in fact taken place. It is only while he is a prey to his "mente, ofuscada por los propósitos de violencia" (III, xi, 421; cf. the reference in III, viii, 396 to his "cabeza ofuscada") that he momentarily accepts "la fiera ley de la barbarie".

All the time a counterforce is operating upon him. Not only, as Johnson notes, his learned principles, which are in the last resort cold and abstract, but his emotions. The deepest level of Santos' personality is his compassion. In the 1929-30 revision his *odio* for Lorenzo Barquero is replaced by compassion; his first response to Marisela is compassion; the main obstacle to their love is her lack of compassion: first for her father, which in Part II, chapter XI, causes Santos to doubt her capacity for emotion; second for her mother, which in Part III, chapter II, produces in him a reaction of serious displeasure. What saves Santos from himself in the end is not merely Marisela's explanation of the real cause of Melquíades' death, but two events. The first is when Pajarote reveals to him by his loyalty that "no era cierto que sólo la bravura armada fuese la ley de la llanura" (III, viii, 397). The second occurs when he recognizes in Marisela at her father's death-bed the capacity for *ternura* which he believed she lacked. These two episodes, both in some sort manifestations of love operating at a deeper level than that of the conscious mind, restore his confidence in the potentiality for good of the *llano*. The existence of this is confirmed by doña Bárbara's change of heart, partly stimulated in her case too by the memory of love — her attachment to Asdrúbal. Love of justice, when it is real, is, as Bernard Shaw reminds us, a moral passion, a thing of the heart not just of the mind. It is restored to Santos by the heart.

Once more, what is our conclusion to be? Are we to agree with Michalski that in Santos "Gallegos sólo logra un personaje de poca densidad, casi un ente alegórico"; or see in him the major Gallegan hero? That he is over-idealized is patent. But he is no mere Prince Charming. His character proceeds from decision to decision, culminating after a brief upsurge of his repressed *barbarie* (which in the end proves to be very much attenuated) in his realization that the real task is not to try to eradicate the evils of the *llano* by violence, but to search out and develop its potentiality for good. He develops, that is, both in personality and insight. More cannot be asked for in a novel of ideas. Ironically, it is in the field of ideas that his character seems less satisfactory. What he achieves he achieves by force. Stripped of rhetoric all that he has done is to replace a bad *cacicazgo* by a good one. Reliance on arbitrary individual authority, which Sarmiento saw as a root cause of barbarism, reasserts itself through Santos by the usual methods. Gallegos was betrayed, by his ambivalent attitude to *barbarie* and to what it represented for the *alma de la raza,* into investing Santos with some of the violent attributes of *machismo* we find in his other heroes. These attributes he half-admired, half-deplored. But the point is this: nowhere else in his work are they shown achieving a constructive purpose, probably because Gallegos knew only too well their real social and political effect. Santos represents the hope that they could be directed into positive channels. But although Gallegos succeeded in harmonizing them in a memorable fictional character, violence and civilizing ideals remain in essence incompatible.

Chapter IV

Marisela and Lorenzo Barquero

"Inventé a Santos Luzardo y a Mariséla, las únicas figuras total-mente mías", Gallegos wrote in *Una posición en la vida* (see note 3), and later in the preface to the 1954 edition of *Doña Bárbara*: "Son respectiva y complementariamente, la empresa que hay que acometer, una y otra vez, y la esperanza que estamos obligados a acariciar, con incansable terquedad" (27). In these remarks he makes two points about Marisela: first, he asserts that like Santos she is a purely fictional character who, in contrast to doña Bárbara, has no basis in reality; second, he emphasizes her symbolism.

Marisela is the simplest of the three major characters in the text, seen as symbols, because nothing of Gallegos' ambivalence about *barbarie* and the *alma de la raza* touches her. She stands absolutely at the opposite extreme to his early pessimism about the potentialities buried in the soul of the Venezuelan people. Her symbolism, like her character, is rectilinear (unlike those of either Santos or Bárbara) and positive. She is "una personificación del alma de la raza, abierta, como el paisaje, a toda acción mejoradora" (II, ii, 209). Gone completely is the vision put forward in 'Las causas', twenty years earlier, of a people "de natural perezoso, incapacitado para el esfuerzo perseverante que exige la labor cívica", gone are the desolate postulates of *Reinaldo Solar*. In their place stands the radiant figure of a young girl: the daughter of *barbarie*, yes; of mixed blood even, since her mother was a *mestiza*; but in terms of the metal-simile of 'Los aventureros' (see p. 13, above) she is "íntegra, pura como un metal nativo". All she needs is to be moulded and polished.

A criticism which might be brought against Marisela is that she is too closely connected to the landowning élite to represent the

Venezuelan people with full conviction. Though a daughter of the *mestiza* doña Bárbara, she is on her father's side a Barquero and Santos Luzardo's cousin. Her marriage to him is no more a symbol of genuine class or racial fusion than was Victoria's in Gallegos' earlier novel *La trepadora*.. By becoming Santos' wife Marisela is only returning to what is already partly her own social position by right. It is noteworthy that Santos pays only condescending attention to the real representatives of the *llanero* women, Melesio's daughters, who are described in patronizing terms. Also Marisela brings to the marriage the lands of El Miedo, thus joining the two properties into an even larger *latifundia.* A final criticism, which hardly needs stressing, is that there is something slightly naive, as the subsequent history of Venezuela has shown, in the completely unqualified optimism of which she is a symbol.

Symbolism apart, Marisela illustrates the innocence, purity and eventually tenderness which Bárbara has lost and can now never fully regain. The culminating scene of Part II, when mother and daughter face one another for the only time, brings this contrast to its peak. Marisela's relapse in Part III, when she returns with her father to La Chusmita, forms, together with Santos' resort to violence, what in dramatic criticism would be called a "third act complication", arousing the apprehensions of the reader so as to make him enjoy the happy ending all the more. Finally, by releasing Santos from his feelings of guilt and remorse about the death of Melquíades, she redeems him morally as he had redeemed her from neglect, ignorance and possible corruption. So the narrative is neatly brought to its harmonious conclusion.

Marisela has then both a symbolic and an autonomous fictional rôle. But are we in the presence of a real person? Two critics especially have discussed Marisela: Molinaro and Chapman. It is appropriate at this point to consider their views. Molinaro suggests that while Santos and Bárbara exert on each other a reciprocal influence for good and evil, Marisela saves both of them at the last through her love. The point is debatable in regard to Bárbara, who is saved from murdering her daughter by the memory of Asdrúbal rather than by any other influence. For the rest Molinaro compares Marisela with Bernard Shaw's Eliza Doolittle and emphasizes that she is redeemed less by Santos' direct teaching and example than by his love. This is indicated by her relapse when her confidence in his love is shaken. Basic for Molinaro, too, is Marisela's experience at her father's death-bed, which through suffering produces in her a spiritual purification.

In contrast to Molinaro's presentation of her as "una mujer de carne y hueso que acciona y reacciona", Chapman stresses the fairy-tale aspect. Santos' action in washing Marisela is a "magic ritual": "baptism and laying on of hands". The *tremedal* is the death symbol threatening the heroine if she breaks faith with love. Finally the magic gift she has received she gives back in the hero's hour of need. At the beginning, Chapman suggests, the Santos-Marisela story is a "male fantasy"; later, with Bárbara as "the wicked mother (read step-mother)" it becomes a "Cinderella triangle". Michalski, inevitably, goes further:

> Gallegos recrea en *Doña Bárbara* un cuento fabuloso, el cual, resumido, suena algo así: El Príncipe Rubio (Santos Luzardo) va al país legendario que tiene usurpado una mala bruja (doña Bárbara) y, después de una serie de pruebas de las cuales sale siempre vencedor, logra rescatar a la Bella Durmiente (Marisela) a quien la bruja tenía hechizada (p. 1016).

It is true that what Gallegos hopefully calls Marisela's "complicada simplicidad" (II, x, 295) is nearer to simplicity of characterization than to complication. But fairy-tale princesses do not evolve: they are psychologically empty, and Marisela is not. Her character develops in three stages. The first and least convincing is from Part I, chapter IX (the first meeting) to Part II, chapter III (the dawn of love). Here the process of change is dramatically telescoped: Marisela is presented initially in animal terms (*bestia arisca, báquiro*) relieved only by her statuesque beauty and the sense of moral caution which makes her raise her hackles when she misunderstands Santos' use of the word *cerciorarse*. But the washing of her face suddenly improves her speech and reveals a hidden "sensibilidad más fina" beneath the grime. She turns out to be already literate, willing to learn, and is easily broken in to civilized behaviour. But now the price must be paid. Primito's visit reveals, in the references to "otro rubor" and "celos de mujer", that a secondary process has already begun in Marisela.

It is essentially this process, of growing love for Santos, which occupies the central phase of her development in Part II, chapters VII and X, culminating in her courageous gesture at the end of the Part. By this point the outward aspect of her changes is largely complete: she is clean and socially acceptable. Now the inner process begins, the change from child-like *inconsciencia* and spontaneity to a more adult recognition of the need to come to terms with life's reality. The operative factor is a traumatic realization: the admission to herself of the repressed knowledge that she is "hija de la Dañera" (III, ii, 341). Ironically it comes just as she has reached the point of *tuteando* Santos.

This is the turning point. At first the consequence is negative. Marisela leaves Altamira and attempts to reject her recently acquired personality. But in vain; there is no going back, like La Catira, to the wild. This is the low point of her trajectory, as she faces the bitterness of her present position and future prospect. What is needed now is "una nueva transformación" which will complete her evolution by adding to her newly-won adult consciousness a measure of that spirituality which was "para Santos Luzardo lo más importante" (II, ii, 210). This is achieved at her father's death-bed. As her mind has been opened earlier, so now "la fuente de ternura" of her heart is opened by suffering, and the *báquiro* of the earlier chapter has achieved mental and emotional maturity. She is ready to save Santos from his remorse and to become his wife.

Gallegos must have been well satisfied with the Marisela-Santos episodes of *Doña Bárbara*, for in the 1929-30 edition they were, as we noted, the only part of the book left largely unaltered. By contrast the vital chapter X of Part I, in which Lorenzo Barquero first appears, was almost completely re-written at that time, with the emphasis changed from Lorenzo to Santos. The latter's long speech, with its key-sentence "Es necesario matar al centauro que todos los llaneros llevamos por dentro" (142), which is of such importance to the work as a whole, replaces a brief reference to the theme made in the first edition not by Santos but by Lorenzo. Lorenzo's two pessimistic speeches which follow were also added in the revision.

There are three approaches to Lorenzo's character: symbolic, representative and technical. His symbolism is vaguer than that of the other major characters. But as was suggested earlier a case can be made out for seeing in him a symbol of the older generation of Venezuela's landowning élite. This generation recognized the need to save the country from *barbarie*, but failed to carry out the task. In practice they supported the dictator Juan Vicente Gómez as a "gendarme necesario" and saw the country's resources fall further into the power of foreign interests. Lorenzo's bitter suggestion that the idealism and vigour of young Latin-American intellectuals is so much *palabrería* and *mixtificación*, and in any case collapses when they reach their thirties, typifies the sense of inferiority which this generation felt as Latins, and their retreat into passivity and racial pessimism.

What Lorenzo represents in the novel, as distinct from what he symbolizes in the nation, is the effect of *barbarie*. He is, in *Doña Bárbara*, its principal victim. On the one hand, in line with so much that we have seen already, he succumbs to atavistic barbarism, the barbarism inherited via his family from the *alma de la raza*: what he refers to as "el bárbaro que estaba dentro de mí" (I, x, 148). On the other hand he is overcome by the external force of barbarism represented by Bárbara. In each case, though Gallegos does not state it directly, the cause is the same: lack of will-power.

His technical rôle in the narrative is thus already clear. He acts primarily as a foil for Santos. His situation had initially been the same, but he lacked the strength of will required to overcome it. In contrast Santos is seen to possess that strength. Also, as Kolb has pointed out, there is a basic moral contrast. Lorenzo fomented the family feud with the Luzardos and encouraged Félix to oppose his father. Lorenzo succumbed at once to Bárbara and, after the birth of Marisela, revealed himself to be utterly devoid of parental responsibility, while Santos attempts to heal the breach between the families, resists Bárbara's wiles and assumes the duty of caring for Marisela. But this is not the whole of Lorenzo's contribution. In addition he has an important place in the novel as an 'interlocutor': a character whose function is to bring out the views of the central figure in conversation with him. It is by means of a conversation between Santos and Lorenzo that Gallegos succeeds in getting the novel's main piece of ideological commentary, its central idea, across to the reader in Part I, chapter X. This avoids the cruder method of reporting his views through the medium of Santos' reflexions in some sort of interior monologue, or of simply writing them into the novel in the form of a direct statement by the author. Finally Lorenzo's prophecy that Santos will meet a fate similar to his own, and his encouragement of Santos to surrender to violence —the memorable "No tengas grima a la gloria roja del homicida" (II, viii, 270)—, by emphasizing the risks and temptations to which Santos is subjected, contribute materially to the development of suspense in the narrative.

Other characters

Where the conflict between the two forces in the novel, positive

against negative, can be seen in its simplest form is in the presentation
of the minor characters. Santos, as we have seen, is not just the
representative of civilization, as Bárbara is in turn more than just an
incarnation of barbarism. But between their respective supporters
the contrast is stark. Bárbara's men are introduced as "una pandilla
de bandoleros, encargados de asesinar a mansalva a cuantos intenten
oponerse a sus designios" (I, i, 36). The faithful *peones* of Altamira
on the other hand are nothing if not idealized.

A feature of the portrayal of Bárbara's henchmen is the further
contrast between Melquíades and Paiba. Both belong to a lower
point on the moral scale than Bárbara, a fact which is of great benefit
to Gallegos' presentation of her. But with respect to each other
they are sharply differentiated. This does not seem to have been
Gallegos' original intention. Melquíades is introduced as "un tipo
de razas inferiores, crueles y sombrías" (I, i, 32), before being
associated, following Gallegos' habitual technique (see p. 73, below),
with his *nahual* the crocodile. Another characteristic nature-
reference associates his voice with the soft sticky mud of the
treacherous quicksands of the *llano*. Finally he is once more
presented in terms of "una maldad buída y fría que traspasaba los
límites de lo atroz" (I, vi, 100). But this is not the reader's final
impression of him, and for a very good reason. When he reappears
in the narrative at the opening of Part III it is in quite a different
guise: that of the perfect henchman, "no un hombre cualquiera sino
uno muy especial" (III, i, 332), dignified by his "lealtad a toda
prueba" to doña Bárbara and his utter contempt for Paiba's squalid
dishonesty. Finally in the 1954 revision Gallegos, careless of his
earlier introduction of Melquíades, added a significant sentence in
praise of "la calma trágica de aquel hombre que nunca se alteraba ni
se apresuraba por nada" (III, i, 333).

Paiba on the other hand is an abject figure, one of those
nineteenth-century villains who mercifully have since disappeared

from respectable literature. Greasy, greedy, obtuse and conceited, he is scorned alike by Santos, Bárbara, Melquíades and Danger. Contrast with him ennobles Bárbara. Santos asserts his *hombría* by mastering him. His murder of Carmelito and Rafael to steal the plumes provides Gallegos with a convenient solution for the problem posed by the death of Melquíades. More than a character Paiba is a crude narrative device.

So too is Juan Primito, for all his impact on the reader's imagination. Drawn from life, as Gallegos wrote in the preface to the 1954 edition, he is one of the most memorable of the author's minor characters. But detached from the symbolism of his *rebullones*, his rôle is purely utilitarian. He acts as an extremely useful interlocutor for Marisela at two critical moments: the dawn of her love for Santos (Part II, chapter III), and the lowest point of its evolution (Part III, chapter VI) when he innocently suggests that her future rôle is that of running a *pulpería* instead of marrying her cousin. Secondly, after the expansion of his rôle in the second edition, he acts as the main instrument by means of which doña Bárbara intervenes in events outside El Miedo. It is largely due to his successive errands that the climax to Part II (the confrontation of Marisela and her mother), the shooting of Melquíades, and the death of Paiba which releases Santos from suspicion, are brought about. To this extent he is a vitally important narrative agent. Kolb shows how Primito also acts as a brilliant foil for his employer: "se complementan en todo", he writes:

> A la soberbia belleza de la mujerona corresponde la fealdad repugnante de su recadero. La voluntad imperiosa e inflexible del ama encuentra su complemento perfecto en la obediencia servil e incondicional del criado. Si ella es cruel, avara y atrevida, él es tierno, generoso y cobarde.

As she hates men, so he is possessed by sexual fantasies of women. As she rejects Marisela, so he becomes father and mother to the child.

Pernalete and the Mondragones need little comment. They are

respectively the pawns of Bárbara when crude violence is required, and her guarantee of immunity. Pernalete himself, the incarnation of a corrupt and arbitrary system of law-enforcement, is a stock figure of the Latin-American novel from Azuela to the present day. Is it significant that he alone of the active representatives of *barbarie* in *Doña Bárbara* is left at the end of the novel to go on as before?

The *peones* of Altamira belong to quite a different human category from Bárbara's supporters. Gallegos' description of the *hombre de la llanura* at the end of Part II, chapter XII, is a pattern of antitheses: "indómito y sufridor", "indolente e infatigable", "indisciplinado y leal", "sensual y sobrio" and so ón. It emphasizes afresh Gallegos' ambivalent vision of the *llano* ("bello y terrible") and its inhabitants (not least doña Bárbara herself with her "hábito del mal" and her "ansia del bien"). But in practice the only one of Santos' men to whom this ambivalence even remotely applies is Pajarote. The others illustrate that mystique of the sturdy, honest countryman with his simple dignity and "authentic" values, in contrast to the degenerate and corrupt city-dweller, which was a legacy of Pereda (and a long tradition) to the *novela de la tierra* in America. Their qualities, like those of Güiraldes' gauchos or Ciro Alegría's Indians, are those of an ideal *hombría* which never, in contrast to the real-life thing, degenerates into mere *machismo*. At the centre is a stoical "voluntad de pasar trabajos", rising to reckless daring in the crocodile hunt. It is accompanied by total loyalty towards each other and towards Santos, frankness, discretion, intelligence and engagingly spontaneous humour, though the latter, as elsewhere in the Latin-American novel until recently, is almost entirely verbal. Humour of situation (except at times unconsciously) is one of the conspicuously absent features of the *novela tradicional.*

Two of Santos' *peones* stand out. In the early part of the novel it is Antonio who emerges most clearly as Santos' unconditional adherent in contrast to the doubting Carmelito. But as the novel progresses his rôle changes. From that of a devoted henchman it becomes that of a representative *llanero* evolving from *barbarie* to *civilización* under Santos' leadership. At first it is Santos who rebukes him for harbouring rancour towards Lorenzo Barquero. At the end it is Antonio who, from a newly acquired standpoint of *sociabilidad,* criticizes his employer for enclosing Corozalito and for ignoring doña Bárbara's rights over her own property. Meantime the man who in Part I, chapter XII had warned Santos sceptically that progress depended on changing the "modo de ser del llanero", in Part III, chapter II, himself suggests enclosing the ranch. "Era la idea del civilizador, germinando ya en el cerebro del hombre de la rutina", comments Gallegos, as we saw already.

With this specialization of Antonio's rôle, that of Pajarote has the opportunity to develop. This was not an unconscious process for Gallegos as the changes made between the first and second editions reveal. Initially Pajarote had been absent from Altamira when Santos arrived and only appeared casually later. Now we see him accorded a very memorable self-presentation which establishes him from the outset as a major secondary character. Two features of his personality contrast with the idealization of Antonio and the other *peones.* One is the irresponsibility which had led him to join in an earlier rebellion for no better reason than to "descansar de la brega con la cimarronera" and because "era hora de repartir los centavos" (II, ix, 285). The other arises from his advice to Santos after the death of Melquíades, which produces one of Santos' major concessions to *barbarie* in that he agrees not to inform the legal authorities but instead to let events take their natural course. To have given Santos such advice would have conflicted with Antonio's new-found sense of responsibility and legality. Hence the shift of emphasis to Pajarote whose views are more elastic.

A third group of characters are the victims of *barbarie*: Lorenzo Barquero, of course, but also the pathetic Mujiquita, similarly described on his second appearance as "una víctima de la barbarie devoradora de hombres" (III, iii, 359). In this case, as in the short story 'Los aventureros', it is noteworthy that a representative of the city intelligentsia is found aiding and abetting the barbarism of the interior. Jesusito, Carmelito and his brother Rafael are also victims. Carmelito, whose reserve and suspicion contrast so effectively with the open-hearted loyalty of Antonio and the gaiety of Pajarote, is doubly so. As his parents were murdered by Pernalete's gang of rustlers, so he and his brother are murdered by Paiba. Carmelito is the ultimate symbol-figure of the effects of violence on the *llano*.

Finally Danger; A. C. Piper in 'El yanki en las novelas de Rómulo Gallegos', *Hispania*, 33 (1950), 338-341, emphasizes that he is not Gallegos' last word on the subject of North Americans. Hardman in *Sobre la misma tierra* (1943) is a much more sympathetic portrait. But Danger is not just a hostile caricature of a Yankee adventurer. His attitude to Bárbara is friendly but deliberately uncommitted. He refuses to be involved in the murder of Apolinar, but exploits his knowledge of it. He commits no acts of violence and plays a waiting game with Marisela rather than actively pursuing her seduction. He is presented in terms of coarse insensitiveness and loutish brutality, based on an unjustified assumption of Anglo-Saxon superiority, rather than as the neo-colonial exploiter of Venezuela's under-development. The key to Gallegos' attitude to Danger appears in Mujiquita's statement "musiú tiene garantías en esta tierra" (II, i, 192) and Antonio Sandoval's confirmation that "el extranjero siempre tiene garantías que le faltan al criollo" (III, vi, 387). What Gallegos objects to is less Danger's personality and activities, both of which are neutralized by Santos, than his privileged position simply as a foreigner, with no corresponding benefit accruing to the country. The fact that he takes his leave at the end of the novel may imply the hope on Gallegos' part that his country would shake off foreign interference.

Chapter V

Symbolism

Symbolism is a basic feature of Gallegos' fictional technique. In *Doña Bárbara* the setting (the *llano* itself), the central characters, many of the episodes, the names of Santos and Bárbara as well as their respective ranches Altamira and El Miedo, and many other elements of the narrative, all possess symbolic meaning. For most of his symbols Gallegos draws on nature, but two exceptions deserve brief mention.

The first of these is the centaur. The key-sentence of the whole novel is Lorenzo Barquero's assertion (I, x, 142): "Es necesario matar al centauro que todos los llaneros llevamos por dentro." The origin of the centaur myth in warlike horsemen, the fact that the centaur has traditionally been seen as the embodiment of irrationality, cruelty and lust, and perhaps the fact that both Galdós and Antonio Machado had used the centaur to represent the worst aspects of Spain's racial heritage, made it a natural choice for Gallegos. He too uses the symbol of the centaur to express the *barbarie*, forming part of the *alma de la raza*, which it was Santos' task to vanquish both in himself and in doña Bárbara.[16]

The other symbol in this category is that of the sphynx, the symbol of inscrutability, which interestingly enough, like the centaur, is part human, part animal — a woman's head on a lion's body. It is the perfect symbol for doña Bárbara, "la esfinge de la sabana", combining feminine beauty and cunning with animal strength and

[16]All the essential facts about centaurs can be found in the Larousse *Encyclopedia of Mythology*. For Galdós and Machado see Gustavo Correa, *El simbolismo religioso en las novelas de Pérez Galdós*, Madrid, 1962, pp. 44 and J. Herrero, 'Antonio Machado's Image of the Centaur', *Bulletin of Hispanic Studies*, 45 (1968), 38-41.

savagery. But more than this it emphasizes her duality. She is both "hecha para el amor" and "mezcla salvaje de apetitos y odio"; eventually, as each side of her nature struggles for mastery over the other, she becomes "esfinge para sí misma" (III, vii, 395). Exactly the same duality is expressed in the reference to the Orinoco and the Guainía (I, iii, 64). The different coloured waters of the two rivers running side by side in the depths of the jungle symbolize the ambivalence deep inside Bárbara's personality.

Such use of natural references of a more or less symbolic kind to illustrate features of personality is an integral part of Gallegos' approach to characterization. The earliest and one of the most typical examples of this occurs on the third page when Melquíades' voice is described as "blanda y pegajosa como el lodo de los tremedales de la llanura". In contrast Marisela is described at the beginning of her education as "todavía silvestre, pero como la flor del paraguatán que embalsama el aire de la mata y perfuma la miel de las aricas" (II, ii, 208). Santos in turn had been seen, after his transplantation as a boy to Caracas, in terms of "la macolla de hierba llanera languideciendo en el tiesto" (I, ii, 51). Gallegos came after the high-water mark of realism and naturalism and tended away from the methods of pseudo-objective description associated with these movements. Equally he was describing the *llano* of the past, different from that which was already being invaded by the railway, the motor car (in which Gallegos himself originally travelled to the *llano*) and the motor-launch. So that, in addition to avoiding traditional realist descriptive methods, he was probably anxious to avoid too much reference to modern factors which were transforming the plains. Hence his recourse to systematic description of the *llano* and its people in terms of the *llano* itself. In doing so he is able not only to employ an effective device as such, but also to include a whole series of new components which widen and deepen our vision of the *llano*. As a further bonus he finds himself even better equipped to preserve in the novel a vision of a world which was disappearing. His avoidance both of new and non-*llano* elements strengthens his portrayal of what was in process of change or still vigorously survived.

More striking than the comparisons are the animals which Gallegos just as systematically associates with numerous characters, so that each, as Michalski notes, comes to have a kind of *nahual* or animal equivalent which expresses his or her personality in semi-symbolic terms. Danger has his *cunaguaro* which expresses his half-playful savagery. Marisela is even more specifically associated with the mare La Catira. Both doña Bárbara and Melquíades are indirectly associated with the crocodile El Tuerto. Bárbara's evil instincts become Primito's imaginary *rebullones*, just as her earlier beauty and purity were associated with the lovely and gentle *gaván* (I, iii, 62), while her superiority and predatory activities were expressed in reference to the *gavilán*.

Not all the symbolism in *Doña Bárbara* is associated simply with character-portrayal. There is, for example, the developed pattern of light/darkness symbolism associated with the theme. The triumph of civilization over barbarism is expressed by this means partly at least in terms of a triumph of light over darkness, with its climax at the end in Part III, chapter XI ('Luz en la caverna') and XIV ('La estrella sobre la mira'). Similarly there are a number of symbolic incidents forming part of the plot itself or closely related to it. Among these a prominent example is Santos' action in wrenching the dagger from the wall of the room in which his father died. This event, to Ramos Calles (*Los personajes de Rómulo Gallegos a través del psicoanálisis*, Caracas, 1969) is one of several features of the book which have strong Freudian undertones of which Gallegos was presumably unconscious. But the conscious symbolism is obvious, and it is even insisted upon in the words which Santos speaks immediately after. No less obvious is the symbolism of Melquíades' failure to capture Cabos Negros, presaging the failure of doña Bárbara's faction in other respects.

More difficult to interpret is the symbolism of the *culebra de aguas* in the last chapter of the novel. Michalski believes the snake to be Bárbara and the *res* to be Lorenzo. Thus the incident is a retrospective symbol. It "unmasks" doña Bárbara's "real self", even after her apparent redemption. If this is so it seems gratuitously cruel, especially since it was added in the second edition. Perhaps instead the incident might be compared with the killing of Jesusito by the jaguar (III, ii, 343). It may be meant to show that, even though its human incarnation has been overcome, the *llano* itself still has reserves of savagery to be vanquished.

A final aspect of symbolism which may be briefly mentioned is Gallegos' use of familiar *llano* things to express abstract ideas. Noteworthy here are the references to the *sufridor* or saddle-cloth, whose name suggests it to Gallegos as a symbol of the *llaneros'* stoicism (II, xii, 316), and to the bitter-sweet *miel de aricas* (II, vii, 263) which aptly symbolizes the pleasure-pain of love.

While there is perhaps a trifle too much symbolism worked into *Doña Bárbara*, so that in the end it becomes rather obtrusive, the fact that all but a couple of the basic symbols are borrowed from the reality of the *llano* itself increases the effectiveness of the method. What could otherwise have been a hollow rhetorical device instead serves to knit the *llano* into the texture of the narrative, presenting it not as a passive picturesque background, but as an active force with a genuinely functional rôle.

Rôle of Nature

One of the standard criticisms of the *novela de la tierra* in Latin America is that Nature tends to usurp the rôle usually assigned in fiction to the central human character. It has even been suggested that in *Doña Bárbara* itself, it is the *llano* which occupies the centre of the stage, dwarfing the other actors. This is certainly an exaggeration. But it is clear that no critical discussion of *Doña Bárbara* would be complete without some reference to Nature.

The first noteworthy feature is that the *llano* is not just a setting for the story in the sense for example in which the Peruvian countryside and *puna* provide one for the novels of Ciro Alegría. It has a rôle in the novel inseparable from that of the other major characters, and like them exists both on the real and the symbolic level. The level of reality is, of course, provided by Gallegos' descriptions of the vast savannah at different seasons of the year, or hours of the day, and in its different moods. Especially memorable here are the description of summer heat and grass fires (II, viii, 264-8) and the great rains of winter (II, xii, 313-315). These are Gallegos' nearest approach to static presentations of scenery. Here, as in other respects, he reacts against the old nineteenth-century traditional techniques, avoiding the minute set-piece descriptions we find for example in Pereda or —closer to Gallegos' own time— in the work of the Mexican novelist Rafael Delgado. He prefers to insert short, striking paragraphs, often only one or two at a time, which suggest by deft touches rather than describe in detail the appearance of the *llano*. Such paragraphs are those for example which describe dusk (I, v, 84), dawn (II, iv, 228) and the daily round at the *queseras* (III, ii, 342-3). This last, with its serene picture of the evening *tonadas* brutally shattered by Jesusito's ghastly death, is a particularly fine example of Gallegos' functional use of description. Functional in another way is his use of the *sequía* as a background —*paysage état d'âme*— for doña Bárbara's last ride back to El Miedo.

Of more technical interest and significance however is the symbolism of the *llano*, together with its contribution to the presentation of the characters associated with it. The symbolism of the *llano* itself reveals the ambivalence that has been noticed elsewhere. The basic impression which Gallegos creates in the reader's mind is that of the savannah as the "devoradora de hombres", linking the natural background closely to doña Bárbara herself. This is the theme of Lorenzo Barquero's speeches at the end of Part I, chapter X ("esta tierra no perdona . . . ¡La maldita llanura, devoradora de hombres! "). It is underlined afresh by Santos' reflection immediately afterwards: "Realmente, más que a las seducciones de la famosa doña Bárbara, este infeliz ha sucumbido a la acción embrutecedora del desierto." Alongside Gallegos' suggestion of a harmful hereditary determinism operating on the characters, derived ultimately from the *alma de la raza*, emerges that of a harmful environmental determinism which is the result of life in the wild. From this standpoint the *llano* is seen as one of the two main founts of *barbarie*.

But this is not always Gallegos' standpoint. We soon notice that he half admires, as well as deplores, what the *llano* represents, even when it is hostile to civilization. It is "bello y terrible a la vez" (I, viii, 117). Its children, while they call to mind the barbarous bloodshed of the Venezuelan nineteenth century, incarnate at the same time the national tradition of heroism. Gallegos cannot bring himself to see in the *llano*, any more than in the *alma de la raza*, a consistently negative factor. Thus little by little, like doña Bárbara, the *llano* is reinvested with positive potentiality. References to its impressiveness and beauty gradually take over from those which had emphasized its savagery, unhealthiness and treachery. It begins to acquire "frescos refugios de sombra" and "plácidos remansos" (II, v, 251). Its evil predators, symbolized in El Tuerto, are overcome. Although later it rebels afresh with grass-fires and the murder of Jesusito by the jaguar, these are mere temporary relapses, like Marisela's or doña Bárbara's jealousy at the end. Despite the episode of the water snake we finally perceive that the *llano*, no less than its inhabitants, is "abierta a toda acción mejoradora".

Actually it is more so than Gallegos suggests. It is far easier to change conditions than to change people. It is only when we notice that in *Doña Bárbara* the change in conditions and the change in characters proceeds at the same pace, that we realize the full extent of Gallegos' optimism.

Style

Gallegos' style has been praised by various critics. Araujo in particular dedicates a useful chapter to 'las palabras mágicas' in his book. He emphasizes the rhythmical qualities and carefully balanced parallelism of Gallegos' prose, his "gusto por la palabra sonora que el espíritu paladea con recocijo" and praises him as a "baquiano de la palabra". Certainly Gallegos cannot be included among those pre-1950 novelists whom E. Rodríguez Monegal has accused of "un desprecio suicida por el lenguaje". He clearly exhibits at intervals throughout *Doña Bárbara* a conscious "voluntad de estilo". But it tends to take the form of rhetorical passages standing out in contrast to the agile, rapid and direct narrative style in which they are embedded.

This is repeatedly visible at the beginning and end of chapters, where Gallegos is especially concerned to set a tone or to round off an effect. The incantatory opening of Part I, chapter III: " ¡De más allá del Cuñaviche, de más allá del Cinaruco, de más allá de la Meta! De más lejos que nunca . . ."; the sonority of the first paragraphs of Part I, chapter VIII; the lyrical description of Marisela's first bath; the poetic apostrophe at the end of Part II, chapter XII; the last paragraph of the novel; these and many more illustrate the truth of Santos Luzardo's statement that he, and by implication Gallegos, are "hombres de una raza enfática, de algún modo aficionados a la elocuencia" (I, x, 142).

In sharp contrast are those taut, striking phrases which bring certain chapters to a sudden dramatic end: "Y avanzó solo con el trágico arrebiate. Solo y convertido en otro hombre" (III, viii, 402); "No matarás. Ya tú no eres la misma" (II, v, 253). A hallmark of

this technique is Gallegos' tendency to begin the last brief paragraph
of a chapter with "y", or less often "pero", apparently linking it to
the preceding one, but in fact marking a sudden change in tone.

Where Gallegos' style is very effective is in his superbly vivid yet
compact brief descriptions such as those of dawn and dusk on the
llano already mentioned, and the long fluid succession of phrases in
apposition beginning "Escombros entre matorrales . . ." and ending
climactically with "esto era el pueblo cabeza del Distrito, teatro de
las sangrientas contiendas entre Luzardos y Barqueros" (II, i, 189-190)
which make up a truly striking evocation of a neglected rural
township of the Latin-American interior. No less visually impressive
is the description of the *sequía* in Part III, chapter XIV, with its
characteristically rhetorical climax: "Doña Bárbara cabalgaba a
marchas forzadas hacia el espejismo del amor imposible." Metaphor
of this kind is however noticeably absent elsewhere and only
occasionally do we see an isolated simile: "las obscuras manos del
arpista al recorrer las cuerdas son como dos negras arañas que tejen
persiguiéndose" (II, ix, 287) or Antonio's charming compliment to
Marisela during their only conversation: "Usted es para el doctor
como la tonada para el ganado, que si no la escucha cantar, a cada
rato está queriendo barajustarse" (III, vi, 388). The deliberate use of
venezolanismos (e.g. *barajustarse*) is of course a stylistic feature
typical of the *novelistas de la tierra* generally.

So far no systematic study of Gallegos' style has been published.
In its absence any conclusion can only be provisional, but it would
probably be correct to class Gallegos and his contemporaries Barrios,
Güiraldes and Mallea as writers who all in their very different ways
attempted to functionalize the highly ornate poetic prose of the
earlier *modernistas*, avoiding its more pronounced limitations for
the practising novelist.

Conclusion

The emergence in the last twenty years of the *nueva novela* in Latin America, with writers like Cortázar, Fuentes, Onetti, Carpentier, Vargas Llosa and García Márquez has produced a radical shift in critical attitudes towards the novels of the 1920 and 1930s. This makes it difficult to achieve an evaluation of *Doña Bárbara* which will meet with general agreement. Supporters of the new novel, under the leadership of E. Rodríguez Monegal, appear to have assumed that it is impossible to appreciate the work of recent figures in Latin-American fiction without denigrating that of older authors. They criticize variously the unambiguous presentation of reality in the novel prior to 1950, the lack of technical innovation, the failure to explore to the full the possibilities of language, and the emphasis on "provincial" *criollista* themes. In reply a few critics have begun the attempt to salvage older fiction by presenting some of its technical features as prefigurations of those which are now fashionable, while others, notably M. P. González, have retorted with root-and-branch denunciations of the latest trends. The result has been a regrettable collapse of critical perspective. Any assessment of *Doña Bárbara* must begin with a plea to reject such misguided exclusivism and to accept the possibility of peaceful co-existence between critics of the *nueva novela* and the *novela tradicional.*

One thing is surely clear: Gallegos' position as one of the three or four major exponents of the *novela criollista* or *telúrica* is unshakeable. His place in the history of the twentieth-century Latin-American novel is therefore assured, though it seems probable that it will not be thought quite so high a place, given the limitations of his *genre*, as has sometimes been suggested in the past. Granting this, it is possible to criticize without hesitation those aspects of his work which

appear aesthetically or ideologically deficient. It has already been
suggested that the ideology of *Doña Bárbara*, though in its time it
had a significant impact, as many writers have testified, now seems
unpersuasive. Both the basis of thought, especially the idea of an
alma or *genio de la raza* (though this was recently resurrected by
Octavio Paz in an essay on Darío), and the historical situation,
which are met with in *Doña Bárbara*, are irretrievably past. There is
a rural problem in Venezuela, but it is subordinate to the wider
problem of the nation as a whole at grips with an excessive dependence
on oil as the national product and with selfish foreign interests
striving to control the economy. In any case enlightened landholding
on *Junker* principles, which is what Santos seems to have in mind, is
not and would not have been a solution. On the wider issue of the
triumph of progressive forces in Venezuela symbolized in the novel,
Gallegos' optimism has proved to be unjustified. Indeed, as R. Caldera
in *Aspectos sociológicos de la cultura en Venezuela* (Caracas 1955,
p. 21) points out, Gallegos himself seemed to relapse into pessimism
in his later work.

In terms of history of literature *Doña Bárbara* is the climactic
work of the *novela criollista* which dominated Latin-American fiction
during most of the first thirty-five years or so of the century. So
much so that when Mariano Latorre, the major Chilean *criollista* and
exact contemporary of Gallegos, defined his aim, he did so in terms
that seem borrowed from Gallegos' central novel. "Mi intención",
he wrote in 1955, "fue la de interpretar la lucha del hombre de la
tierra por crear civilización en territorios salvajes" (cit. Homero
Castillo, *El criollismo en la novelística chilena*, Mexico 1962, p. 38).
Aesthetically, too, *Doña Bárbara* is an end-product. The comment
of Uslar Pietri on Gallegos, that "No hay novelista grande menos
renovador y audaz en lo formal y lo técnico", taken up and
developed by Liscano, is basically justified. Gallegos was not
seriously concerned with exploring new possibilities in fictional

technique. When here and there in his work a character, a scene, or a stylistic feature seems to portend the *nueva novela*, it is by accident. The blemishes associated with his manner of writing in *Doña Bárbara* —mechanical plot-structure, a too undisguised approach to commentary, especially psychological commentary, unsubtle use of symbolism, a certain element of rhetoric— have all been frankly indicated in the foregoing pages. But they are blemishes which are more apparent when the novel is studied than when it is read. Its impact then, as a totality, is memorable. *Doña Bárbara*'s qualities, unity, economy, pace, suspense, immediate appeal, in short, the traditional qualities of the direct narrative method, are the opposite of those which have since come into fashion. But to call them "primitive" as Vargas Llosa did recently in *Books Abroad* (44, 1970, p. 8) is as unhelpful as it would be to dismiss without argument Vargas Llosa's technical devices as mere gimmicks. Gallegos will survive the current attempt to re-interpret the task of the novelist in terms of *hazañas verbales* with his reputation, however modified, substantially intact.

Bibliographical Note

E. Subero has edited *Contribución a la bibliografía de Rómulo Gallegos*, Caracas, 1969, massive but weak on work in the U.S.A. and Europe. My own 'Rómulo Gallegos, suplemento a una bibliografía', *Revista Iberoamericana* 75 (1971), 447-457, attempts to fill the main gaps.

Biography
1.   Liscano, Juan. *Rómulo Gallegos, vida y obra.* Mexico, 1968, has the basic facts. There is no fully adequate biography.

General Studies
2.   Dunham, Lowell. *Rómulo Gallegos, vida y obra.* Mexico, 1957. The best introduction to Gallegos' work as a whole.
3.   Damboriena, Ángel. *Rómulo Gallegos y la problemática venezolana.* Caracas, 1960. A fuller study spoiled by an arbitrary approach to characterization.

Critical Studies
4.   Araujo, Orlando. *Lengua y creación en Rómulo Gallegos.* 2nd edition, Caracas, 1962. A compact and convincing study with special attention to technical features.
5.   Liscano, Juan. *Rómulo Gallegos y su tiempo.* Caracas, 1969. The nearest approach to a really modern, sophisticated critical study.
6.   Castanien, Donald G.,   'Introspective Techniques in *Doña Bárbara*', *Hispania*, 41 (1958), 282-288. Examines helpfully Gallegos' use of interior monologue.
7.   Chapman, A.,   'The Barefoot Galateas of Bret Harte and Rómulo Gallegos', *Symposium*, 18 (1964), 332-341.   The best article on Marisela.

8.   Englekirk, John E.,   'Doña Bárbara. Legend of the *Llano*', *Hispania*, 31 (1948), 259-270. Indispensable for the circumstances of composition.

9.   Johnson, Ernest A., 'The Meaning of *Civilización* and *Barbarie* in *Doña Bárbara*', *Hispania*, 39 (1956), 456-461. Postulates love as the bridge between the two concepts.

10.   Jones, C. A. *Three Spanish American Novelists.* Diamante 17, London, 1967. Sharply criticizes the ending of *Doña Bárbara.*

11.   Kolb, Glen L.,   'Aspectos estructurales de *Doña Bárbara*', *Revista Iberoamericana*, 53 (1962), 131-140. Illustrates convincingly the structural symmetry of the work and contains valuable character studies.

12.   Michalski, André S.,   '*Doña Bárbara*; un cuento de hadas', *Publications of the Modern Language Association of America*, 85 (1970), 1015-1022. Attacks any realist interpretation. The most important recent article.

13.   Molinaro, Julius,   '*Doña Bárbara y Pigmalión*', *Quaderni Iberoamericani*, 3 (1956), 212-215. Useful for Marisela.

14.   Rivas Rivas, J., 'Santos Luzardo', *Revista Nacional de Cultura*, 127 (1958), 23-42. The best analysis of Santos.